LIFE *in* COLOUR

LIFE *in* COLOUR

HOW ANIMALS SEE THE WORLD

MARTIN STEVENS

WITNESS
BOOKS

CONTENTS

INTRODUCTION

In springtime, the British countryside is awash with colour: carpets of bluebells cover the woodland floor; brightly coloured robins, bullfinches and other birds dash back and forth to their nests; and insects, sporting a dazzling variety of hues, buzz all around. Colour is everywhere in nature, and it signifies the diversity of life better than almost anything else.

To us, the world can be a stunning place, but what is it like for other animals, and what functions does colour serve? The great variety of appearances in nature is no coincidence, for colour plays a critical role in practically every aspect of animal behaviour. It is key to attracting a mate, recognising individuals and species, deterring predators, and tricking others to do things that they might not otherwise intend.

The vibrancy of nature goes hand in hand with the variety of ways that animals perceive the world. For colour is not, as we often tend to assume, a property of an object itself, but rather a sensation imparted on animals as a consequence of how their vision and brain work. When we see a rainbow, we perceive a beautiful array of colours. This happens because white light from the sun passes through water droplets in the sky, which split the light into different wavebands, like a prism. Through the presence of several types of cells in our eyes – the cones – our vision is capable of capturing light of different wavelengths. Our brain colours different parts of the spectrum with a sensation of a given hue: red for longwave light, blue for shortwave light, and so on; but, the wavebands of light themselves have no intrinsic colour. Animals with different types of colour vision therefore should not see the world or, indeed, a rainbow quite like we do. Were a sea lion to gaze out of the water at a rainbow over the

Beauty is in the eye of the beholder – not all animals can appreciate the colour of a carpet of bluebells in spring.

ocean, it would see no colour at all. A dog running along the beach would see the blue- and yellow-type hues, but not the pinks or reds that we do. On the other hand, a gull flying over the waves might see all the colours we sense, plus a variety more besides. Colour is in the eye of the beholder.

The costumes of animals are rarely uniform blocks of a single colour. Instead, they come in all sorts of patterns and shapes, from the intricate eyespots on the wings of an emperor moth to the zig-zag markings on an adder. To see such patterns, animals must perceive spatial information in their environment, using sets of cells in their vision that form an image. This is normally undertaken using specific organs – the eyes. Sure enough, eyes have evolved multiple times during the history of life and come in myriad forms. We are most familiar with the camera-type eyes of humans and other vertebrates, with a single opening and lens, where light is focused onto the back of the eye – the retina, on which an image is formed. Yet eyes vary substantially. Insects, for example, possess an assortment of compound eyes, made up of thousands of tiny lenses, each projecting an image of a small part of the world onto the light-sensitive cells below. To them, the world looks rather more blurry.

Other types of vision are truly hard to comprehend. Small marine molluscs called chitons have hundreds of eyes all over their body, as do giant clams, with sparkling eyes distributed in lines along the outer mantle. Most bizarrely of all, some animals appear to be able to perceive crude differences in lighting, and even objects, without eye structures at all. They have sets of visual cells spread out over their whole body. Brittle stars have such an arrangement, and can orientate towards shelter in this way. Quite what the world looks like to these animals is hard to imagine.

With such an abundance of eyes to see the world, and so much variation in how creatures perceive light, it is, perhaps,

Some armour-plated molluscs have simple eyes distributed all over their body, like Ferreira's chiton from British Columbia.

Overleaf: In Costa Rica, this red-eyed tree frog adopts green hues for camouflage and red for communication.

unsurprising how widely colour patterns are used in nature, and the diversity in appearances they take – unsurprising, but magnificent, for colour in nature is what helps animals to stay alive, find food and reproduce. What's more, the diversity in how animals see their environment means that creatures living in the same place can perceive things quite differently. Groups of animals, for example, can communicate with one another using colours or patterns of light that are invisible to rivals or dangerous predators. Such private channels of communication can be hidden from us too, with their use of ultraviolet or polarised light. The natural world is one of technicolour, but each creature perceives only a snapshot of what's out there.

Not all colour in nature has a function, yet there is no doubt that the diversity in hues and patterns is frequently involved with a specific task, often in some form of communication. To begin with, colour plays a major role in enabling species to recognise one another, including to prevent mating with the wrong species, or even for animals to recognise specific individuals, be they friend or foe. Appearances are also of great importance to attract a suitable mate and convince a reluctant suitor that the bearer is up to standard.

On the other hand, colour can be central to signifying dominance and controlling rivalries, not just for mating, but in access to food or other resources. In many species, colour serves a critical function in defence, from warning predators that an animal is defended with toxins or spines, to camouflage, in order to hide in plain sight. Last but not least, colour is widely employed in deception, from sneaking past dominant rivals to get closer to potential mates, to tricking others into raising the young of another species as their own. Variety is the spice of life, and in nature that is exemplified perhaps no better than with the uses and diversity of colour.

Deceiving the eyes of both predators and prey, this satanic leaf-tailed gecko from Madagascar takes camouflage to its highest level.

CHAPTER ONE

FRIEND OR FOE

Our planet's wildlife is spectacularly rich in colour – witness the striking markings on a blue-ringed octopus or the vivid green body and bright red eyes of a tree frog – but these colours are not there simply to look pretty. They serve a vital purpose, for colour is a key ingredient in the many remarkable and sometimes sinister ways that animals behave and how they influence the behaviour of others.

Communicating species identity is an important process in evolution, the inhabitants of coral reefs exemplifying the diversity of different colour patterns as well as any forms of life, not least in the myriad fish species that exist there. Decorated in yellows and blues, pinks and reds, reef fish dazzle scuba divers who descend into their vibrant world. Some fish peep out of crevices in the coral, while others

Coral reefs teem with colour, and many fish use bright hues to communicate, including the towbar anemonefish, seen here shoaling alongside lyretail anthias in the Red Sea, Egypt.

brazenly swim in and around the habitat in great shoals. The most widely known, perhaps, are the clownfish. Of these, the most instantly recognisable species are the orange clownfish and the ocellaris clownfish, two species with the classic orange body and white stripes, often fringed with black outlines. They are colourful and charismatic (and make for good cartoon characters).

The clownfish are a group of 30 or so species whose origins date back between 10 and 20 million years, in a region around Southeast Asia and northern Australia. Today, they still inhabit reefs throughout this area. On hatching, larval clownfish enter a short planktonic phase, floating around in the ocean currents before juvenile fish search out and settle on suitable coral reefs. How they find the right locations is remarkable in itself. In many cases, they quite literally smell the coral reefs, or locate them based on odours from terrestrial trees that grow nearby, often on the shore. These provide reliable cues as to the likely existence of a good place to call home. Juvenile fish also locate reef habitats based on their noise. We don't tend to appreciate it, but coral reefs are noisy places and many fish and other animals communicate with sound, not to mention creating a variety of noises as they fight, feed and generally go about their everyday lives.

Once on a suitable patch of reef, the fish locate a specific creature – the sea anemone. (This has given them one of their other common names, the anemonefish.) Clownfish are reliant on sea anemones for protection, and the adults always live with them. The stinging cells of the host offer safety from predators, and even the odd tasty morsel that the fish can cheekily steal. Quite how the fish avoid being stung themselves is not fully known, but it's thought they secrete a layer of mucus on their skin that protects them from being harmed. They also undergo an acclimatisation period whereby they gradually increase contact with the host anemone, until they can swim freely among its stinging tentacles. (It looks rather like they are dancing into the anemone.) There's little doubt that the clownfish benefit from their home, with some estimates suggesting that clownfish live up to six times longer than similar-sized fish species that do not use anemones. To add to that, the clownfish eggs are laid close to the anemone, and they too get protection.

Clown anemonefish from Bali, Indonesia, take refuge in an anemone.

Overleaf: Clown (top left), Clark's (bottom left), saddleback (top right) and tomato (bottom right) anemonefish from the Indo-Pacific show a variety of costumes that potentially help them to recognise their own species.

In return, the anemone seems to benefit in a number of ways too. The body movements of the fish lead to increased water flow across its home, and the clownfish will often clean its host and aggressively drive away potential predators. It is a classic case of mutualism, where both species benefit from the relationship.

Across the 30 species, clownfish are remarkably diverse in their costumes. Their base colour spans red, brown, orange and even black, marked with up to three distinct body stripes arranged in a variety of shapes and orientations. Size is also variable, with some species just 6 or 7 centimetres long, while others can be more than 15 centimetres. Colourful pigments of various types enable clownfish to produce their striking colours, and special cells and tissue structures that reflect light, especially white light, make the stripes stand out. Juveniles sometimes have more stripes than the adults, and lose some of them as they mature.

The function of the stripes and base colour and their variation among species is not entirely clear. On one level, some appearances may aid in camouflage, blending into parts of the reef and breaking up the body outline. As with other reef fish, given the multi-coloured nature of the habitat, being colourful does not necessarily preclude concealment, and the appearance of the fish may even act as a warning to predators not to attack, since the clownfish cohabit with a dangerous ally. Potential predators might learn that the markings on a clownfish are a warning that they could be stung by the host, should they be foolish enough to venture too close. The best evidence to date, however, is that the coloration acts, at least in part, as communication between the fish, and specifically in recognising their own species.

Scientists have shown that the stripe patterns found on species living in different places depend on the diversity of other clownfish in the neighbourhood, and in turn, what those other species look like. Fish species living in the same area tend to use dissimilar colours and stripe patterns – this is to be expected when colour is used in recognising species. The distinctive stripes help individuals to associate correctly with their own kind, and possibly also help reinforce any dominance hierarchy and other types of social communication. In clownfish society, the breeding pair is dominant over the other non-breeding fish living together in the anemone. Not only that, sometimes several clownfish species occupy the same parts of the reef and even share the same anemone. These different species also have a pecking order, with one species dominant over another. When this happens, those species that are likely to share anemones also tend to be different in appearance, so that they don't mix each other up.

* * *

Of course, this use of colour and patterns for species recognition and identifying individuals is not exclusive to fish. Primates also have a rich variety of behaviours and interactions stemming from their appearance, not least that of each other's faces.

The forests of Central and West Africa are rich in primates, not only iconic ape species such as chimpanzees, bonobos and lowland gorillas, but also a range of colourful monkeys, including the guenons. Guenons live in groups, and not just of their own kind, but often with several different species, resting, feeding and travelling together. They are hard to observe, generally living high up in the canopy, where they interact using a variety of sounds and facial expressions while feeding on fruits, seeds and insects. Each species has its own channels of communication but, as might be expected from living together, individuals from different species can understand each other, especially alarm calls.

BEHIND THE SCIENCE

Animals go to great lengths to identify their own species from other similar ones. There are many reasons for this. One is that convincing a potential partner that you are a worthy mate by performing elaborate courtship rituals is a huge investment, so a lot of time and energy would be wasted if you end up trying to impress individuals of the wrong species. Should different species end up mating, then a whole raft of problems may arise: fertilisation is not successful, for example, or any resulting offspring are not viable because they might incur any number of maladies that render them unable to survive or reproduce themselves. In short, hybridising is not usually something evolution favours, so species have evolved mechanisms to avoid it.

Being species that are closely related and living side by side, there is a real risk that different guenon species might breed with one another, but they have a wonderful way of preventing this. During their evolution, the group has undergone extreme diversification in face patterns and colours, giving them some of the most distinct and variable faces on the planet. The various species have a wonderful range of eye tufts, colourful face marks, white noses and eyebrow patches. Some look like they've been painted by a make-up artist – the red-eared guenon has a blue face mask around the eyes, light yellow cheek tufts, a white chin ruff, and a red nose and snout. Others, such as red-tailed and putty-nosed monkeys, have a nose so bright it looks as if it's been dipped into a pot of ultra-white paint.

Communicating identity, status and intent is often achieved with facial colours and expression in primates, such as in this red-shanked douc langur, from Vietnam.

As with the clownfish, species of guenon monkey living in the same location look very different in facial appearance. Essentially, they need to differ when there is a greater risk that they'll meet one another, or indeed share the same group, making it easier for them to tell each other apart. We don't know exactly what has driven the evolution of specific facial features of each guenon species. Why do some, for example, have a blue eye mask and others a white nose? One thing is clear, however: some species have just one salient feature in order to recognise their own kind, such as the white nose of a putty-nosed monkey, while other species rely on a combination of features. Mona monkeys, for instance, recognise each other by a yellow forehead and cheek tufts, a pink muzzle and a blue face mask. Faces may also be used to distinguish one individual from another, since facial appearance can vary within a species. Yet faces don't reliably differ with age or sex, so they don't seem to play a role in courtship. Facial features are used in identifying species and individuals, although it's not entirely clear why different guenon species go to such extremes, and have the striking faces that they do. It must have something to do with standing out in the crowd and accentuating their facial expressions.

* * *

In the forests of Laos and Vietnam lives an endangered primate whose appearance is so remarkable it is sometimes referred to as the 'costumed ape'. Red-shanked douc langurs are monkeys, rather than apes, however, and they live in groups of 15 or more males and females up in the forest canopy. Each langur has dark charcoal-grey fur over its head and body, spreading into white along the ends of the arms, a bit like hairy gloves. The legs are rich brown-red, almost as if each individual had pulled on a pair of trousers, and a long white tail dangles down from the branch it is sitting on, but it is the face that is its most remarkable feature. Two large brown eyes are set into a mask of orange, which looks as if it had been dusted with make-up, and eyebrows highlighted in blue. A ring of long white hair around the face finishes the look.

Groups travel through the forest looking for good spots to eat, where they forage on young leaves and flowers. Sometimes they will settle in to feed for several days before moving on. Living in a group of up to 50 individuals, however, requires a certain etiquette and pecking order to be adhered to. Social interactions are important, with each group member acquiring a different status and dominance rank that dictates its level of influence. That's where its face comes in. Maintaining dominance ranks, and just keeping the group together, requires being able to recognise individuals, and the face of each monkey is different from all the others in the troop. Furthermore, langurs supplement the colour of their masks with a variety of facial expressions, including combinations of gaping mouths, chin thrusts, baring their teeth and flexing the eyebrows. Different versions of these are used from mating through to play.

Communication, however, may not have been the original driver for colour vision and coloured faces. While the lives of langurs and guenons are greatly influenced by colour, many mammals – including a number of primates, such as certain species of lorises and lemurs – lack what we would consider good colour vision. They cannot distinguish colours that to us appear as reds, oranges, yellows and greens. Instead, the world effectively appears as shades of blue and green-yellow. Yet langurs, along with many other primates, have evolved the ability to tell apart reds, yellows and greens, and much of the driving force for this was foraging. In the tropics, the young leaves preferred by the monkeys

tend to be red and yellow, as are many flowers and fruit. Being able to see these colours is therefore a major advantage. As a consequence of evolving better colour perception for finding food, the monkeys were also freed up to use a range of colours to communicate, leading in one way or another to their curious faces. The yellow-orange colour of the mask stands out noticeably to other monkeys against the green forest background, and probably enhances the clarity of their curious facial expressions. This is common in nature: animals and plants frequently use colours to help individuals or particular body features stand out from their surroundings.

Within groups of clownfish and guenons, individuals display some differences, but variety occurs mostly from one species to the next. While langurs recognise individuals based mainly on variation in the colour patterns they display, some animal groups show even greater individual differences, and this can be crucial for social interactions to work.

Many wasps, especially the common highly social species with which we are most familiar, are keen predators, actively flying around looking for food, and so expose themselves to a range of threats, from predatory birds to dragonflies. Their bright yellow and black coloration, therefore, warns these enemies not to attack or risk being on the receiving end of the wasp's strong jaws and painful sting. What's even more intriguing is how they conduct their lives, and how colours and patterns are important in keeping the peace in wasp colonies. The various worker wasps, along with the dominant queen, live together and perform the tasks needed to protect the nest, find food and raise the next generation. To achieve all this requires

In the forests of Central and West Africa, several species of guenon may mingle in the same group. The characteristic faces of red-tail (top left), De Brazza's (top right), lesser white-nosed (bottom left) and mona (bottom right) monkeys help them mate only with their own kind.

a reliable system of communication, and some species of wasps have a surprising one.

The golden paper wasp is widespread in North America, especially common around woodland where it can source the material needed to make its paper nests. Most individuals have the typical black and yellow warning colours, but the patterns and colours on faces and abdomens vary enormously, with countless shades of brown and black, together with spots, stripes and other markings. It is a social species, living in a colony with a queen and around 200 adult female workers. The colony is usually founded by several potential queens who fight aggressively to take the top role. The winning queen is the most dominant individual and monopolises the production of young, while the losers fight for their place in a dominance hierarchy.

Next in the pecking order will become queen and take over should the monarch die. As the workers are produced and mature, they also take on a given rank in the hierarchy. It determines the role played in the nest and how much aggression an individual receives from the other workers.

For a hierarchy of this sort to work, it is essential that wasps are able to identify each other, and this is achieved by looking at one another's faces. Should any worker not be recognised, because it has novel face markings, it is subject to much more aggression; that is, until the point at which they become familiar to their nest mates. Clearly, for high-ranking wasps, this helps maintain their position in the colony without always having to fight for it. In turn, the benefit for lower ranks is that they suffer reduced aggression, provided they are recognised.

Other species of wasp that are broadly similar, but have just one queen and no such dominance hierarchy, have much less variable faces. What's more, when tested in experiments, they are not very good at remembering face patterns – because normally they don't have to. In the golden paper wasp, the diversity in faces, and a good memory for recognising them, is driven by the need to maintain a strict rank. In some regards, it is surprising that wasps remember and recognise faces, not because they have relatively small brains compared to primates, but because the compound eyes of insects do not offer great resolution or ability to see detail. However, calculations of the size of the face and abdominal markings, as well as how effectively wasp eyes may resolve pattern sizes, suggest that wasps should be able to see these patterns, although not from very far away – within a few centimetres.

* * *

Golden paper wasps in Arizona, USA, construct a nest and live together under a strict hierarchy. The rank of each individual is revealed to others by its facial pattern.

The faces of golden paper wasps reveal a variety of colours
and patterns that help individuals to recognise one another.

While reducing aggression in a social system through the use of colour signals can be helpful in maintaining order, for some animals, aggression can come from other sources, leading to striking and sometimes deceitful ways to prevent it. In these cases, deterrence reflects a balance that changes over time between attracting attention when it is valuable and avoiding confrontation. Giving off the right signals at the right time must also take into account other risks, not least being seen by unwanted eyes. Striking the right balance regularly occurs in the context of mating, when animals, especially females, frequently need to trade off successful reproduction with avoiding, not necessarily predators, but over-amorous males.

Knowing who to mate with and who to avoid is an issue many animals face. This does not only apply to correct species identification, but also in telling apart males and females. To this end, the sexes within a species often look very different, particularly in their colours and patterns. One explanation for such differences is mate choice: males must dazzle and impress discerning females. Damselflies do things differently.

Damselflies are no less colourful than many other adult insects, but they have more than two colour types, i.e. one for males and one for females. After spending sometimes years as aquatic larvae, adults emerge and live for just a few days or weeks. In that comparatively short time, they must reach maturity, successfully mate and lay their eggs in and around sources of water. Competition for mates is not so much akin to the elegant displays of many birds, but more of a mating scramble. There is intense competition among males, so females are harassed by males desperate for success. Many get hurt, waste lots of energy avoiding males and even risk being seen by predators that may be attracted to the mêlée. Some avoid these encounters by the clever use of colour.

The blue-tailed damselfly is a common species in Europe, with different colour forms signifying its sex and readiness to mate.

The rich variety of colours seen in damselflies, from deep reds to bright blues, is produced by a variety of mechanisms that are flexible in how they work and combine. Some colours are made by pigments in the hard body cuticle and in cells just below this, and these selectively absorb certain wavelengths of light, leaving other wavelengths to produce hues such as reds or yellows. Other colours, especially blues, are produced by granular structures that form as the insects moult. They interfere with incoming light so that only certain wavelengths are reflected back. These processes allow damselflies to produce a kaleidoscope of colours. It also enables a number of species to exist in multiple colour varieties. Females, in particular, may exist as several colour types. Being an ancient group of insects, dragonflies and damselflies have had

An immature violet form of the blue-tailed damselfly – her hue signals that she is not ready for courtship.

ample opportunity to evolve excellent colour vision to perceive these different varieties.

The blue-tailed damselfly is abundant in Britain from spring to early autumn. The male of this species has, as the name suggests, a beautiful bright blue tip on the end of its otherwise dark abdomen. The same vivid blue markings are set alongside black on the main body and even across the eyes. However, colour changes with age. The body colour of immature males can be almost emerald green, but, for this species, it is the females that vary the most. They exist in at least five different colour varieties, ranging from the same blue found in males to violet, yellow-green, and even reddish-brown, with or without the colourful tail tip. Like males, female colours also vary with reproductive status:

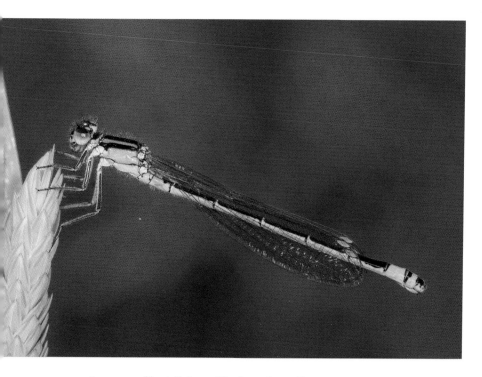

A common bluetail damselfly from Australia.

Overleaf: Dragonflies and damselflies have excellent colour vision, well-suited to telling apart the multitude of colour forms.

they can be blue, brown or yellow-green when they reach maturity. Why do these females vary so much? A large part of the answer is to avoid the unwanted attention of males.

Male damselflies tend to focus on those female colour types that are most common and overlook rarer forms. So, a female will be harassed less if she is blue, when most other females are green. Over time, the frequency of colour types can vary from one to the other depending which is in vogue, along with the anti-harassment protection they provide, but, by mixing things up, the intensity of male pressure can be lowered, at least for some.

The colour of immature females, usually violet or pink, also protects them from harassment. It's a sign that these females are not yet ready to breed. Once they do mature, females with the blue male-like form are pestered less than those that take on the distinct female form. However, there's likely more to it than simply to avoid pestering. On the one hand, yellow-brown and brown forms probably benefit from being less detectable to predators, such as birds, as their drab bodies blend in with their background. On the other hand, the blue forms can be more easily seen against, say, green reeds by potential mates, but risk being spotted by predators. So a female's colour strikes a balance between being identified by potential mates when she is ready to breed, not being seen by potential mates when she wants to avoid being harassed or when she is immature, and not being eaten by predators.

Some wily females go one better. They delay any colour change until the very last minute, and one such species is the Australian common bluetail. Males are bright blue, and many females are brown or dull green, but some females are also blue. These blue females resemble males and, indeed, can effectively fool males that they are also males and so avoid being harassed. Instead, they can forage and live in relative peace. When it comes to the time to mate, however, they perform a clever trick. They simply change colour to a typical female green or brown form. The transformation takes just 24 hours, an astonishingly quick modification, and these females are just as likely to mate successfully as those that never try to mimic males at all. So, colour diversity in damselflies is dependent on sex and the individual and can vary over time.

***

All these animals – clownfish, guenons, wasps and a host of others – use colours that we can see, so we can observe directly any differences between species, sexes and individuals just as they can. Many animals, though, use channels of communication that are hidden from us.

Tropical coral reefs are bursting with colour, yet we perceive these environments very differently from many of the reef's inhabitants, who see colours and light in a variety of ways. Some species of reef fish have excellent colour vision, comparable to or even better than our own. Other reef residents, including species of shrimp, lack colour vision at all, seeing their environment in shades of grey. The vibrancy of the reef and its creatures depends on the eyes of the beholder. This matters in visual communication.

The Ambon damselfish is a species found on reefs around the Indo-Pacific region and is especially well known on the coasts of Queensland, Australia. Their vivid yellow colour is actually a relatively good match with the colourful reef environment. We often assume that the blues and yellows of reef fish make them stand out, especially when seen out of context; yet, the blue can blend in well with the watery backdrop, and many corals and sponges have a yellow hue.

Ambon males are very territorial and chase away rivals from their patch, especially when trying to keep tabs on females who they hope will breed within their area. Should a rival male come close, the territory owner will turn side on and display his body and fins as a threat. If that doesn't work, he chases the gatecrasher away and even delivers a nasty bite. Yet some fish look exactly alike and swim right through without being challenged. Ambon damselfish are known to communicate with a range of sounds, but this is not the case here. The intruder is, in fact, another

By using ultraviolet face patterns, hidden from predators, male lemon (top) and Ambon (bottom) damselfish from Indonesia can detect rivals intruding into their territories.

species – a lemon damselfish. To us, it's almost indistinguishable from the Ambon, but it is actually very different, displaying colours and patterns hidden from our eyes.

BEHIND THE SCIENCE

To uncover how the damselfish are communicating, we use modern advances in imaging technology that enable us to record videos and photographs in parts of the light spectrum that we miss, most notably ultraviolet light. Humans, at least those who are not colour blind, see colours in nature by detecting different wavelengths of light using three receptors in our eyes, called the cone cells. Of these, one is sensitive to relatively shortwave 'blue' light, another to mediumwave 'green' light, and the third to longwave 'red' light. The colours we see depend on how various wavelengths of light stimulate these cells. Likewise, given our visual range, most conventional cameras and video recorders detect colours in a similar way to us and cover the same overall range of 'visible light'. Human vision is incomplete, though. Many other animals can see ultraviolet light, to which we are blind. Our lens cuts out ultraviolet wavelengths before they reach the retina, and we have no cells in our eye dedicated to measuring this spectrum of light. Those animals that do perceive ultraviolet have special receptors in their eyes specifically for detecting these very short wavelengths, but with special cameras, designed to detect ultraviolet light, we can also record patterns and colours that show up in this part of the spectrum. They can reveal hidden worlds.

Seen under ultraviolet, sets of intricate markings appear on the faces of the damselfish. These vary between the two species, and damselfish can see them. The fish have cells in their eyes that detect this part of the light spectrum, as well as having cells that record more familiar colours. So, the resident Ambon can see

UV markings act like facial fingerprints on the lemon (top) and Ambon damselfish, with markings on the face and body revealing identity (bottom).

that the lemon damselfish is another species and not a threat to his group of females or his territory. He can safely leave the visitor alone. These damselfish also differentiate between individuals of the same species based on their ultraviolet face patterns. The fish learn to recognise the specific markings found on different faces, and this may help them to further refine their behaviour, depending on whether a fish is a known rival or an unknown quantity.

The reason damselfish communicate with ultraviolet face markings is probably to remain below the radar and avoid attracting predators. Their bright yellow colour is good camouflage against the reef, but adding contrasting colours to attract mates and communicate with others of the same species might compromise this disguise and heighten the risk of being seen. After all, damselfish are the perfect size to make a tasty meal for something like a rock cod or a coral trout, but these large predatory fish cannot see ultraviolet; they lack the right receptor cells. What's more, owing to the very short wavelengths involved, ultraviolet light also scatters quickly and cannot be seen easily from more than a few metres away. By hiding their facial recognition patterns in colours that predators can't detect and that only work at short range, the Ambon damselfish can manage potential conflicts without compromising its wider safety.

* * *

The ability to see and communicate at the ultraviolet end of the light spectrum is surprisingly common in the animal kingdom, with creatures as diverse as birds and bees adopting it in a variety of tasks, but it is not the only property of light that we cannot appreciate directly. There is another communication channel that is even more alien to us.

The forests of South and Central America are home to an abundance of stunning butterflies, including the *Heliconius* or passion-vine butterflies. There are about 50 different species, and these butterflies vary greatly from one to the next. There are those that sport blue, white and black patterns while others have wings decorated in reds and yellows.

While active during the day, these butterflies float through the undergrowth and across clearings, their slow and ponderous flight helping to advertise their striking warning colours to would-be predators. Being toxic to animals like birds, these insects are best avoided when other more palatable food sources are available. The warning patterns vary from one species to the next, but several groups of *Heliconius* species resemble or mimic one another, and looking alike has benefits for all. It makes it easier for predators to learn and to avoid individuals of all those species, because those enemies need to learn fewer colour patterns than if all the species looked different. As a result, the birds eat fewer toxic prey animals and can target insects that hopefully won't give them an upset stomach. In turn, individual butterflies of each species are less likely to be attacked, and they share the risk of educating predators.

The problem for many *Heliconius* butterflies is that, if two species look alike, how do individuals know which are appropriate mates? There must be something that prevents them courting the wrong species; and part of the answer is hidden from our eyes. Striking markings adorn the wings of some species, such as the crimson and white splashes of colour on the otherwise dark wings of the 'red postman', but they are most vivid when seen under ultraviolet light. At the same time, the butterflies have evolved a highly effective visual system for discriminating different types of ultraviolet colours. They not only have receptors for seeing light that conveys colours that to

Six species of Heliconius *butterfly from South America. The bottom four species are forest dwellers with blue iridescent wing scales that reflect patterns in polarised light. The top two species are from more open areas and lack this.*

us appear as blues or reds, but some *Heliconius* species have also evolved not one but two types of receptor for seeing ultraviolet. In fact, the situation is even more interesting, since it is only the females that have evolved this extra ability. Males are stuck with just one receptor for the task. Female butterflies can be particularly good at telling species apart based on the UV component found on their white or pale yellow wing patches. These ultraviolet wing signals are important in approaching the correct species in order to mate. Likewise, birds have similar limitations as male butterflies. They can see ultraviolet light, but have just the one cell type to detect it so, although they have excellent vision, birds find that the toxic butterflies and their mimics look alike. But the female butterflies can see through the disguise.

Recognising a suitable mate is a problem solved not just by the use of colour. Another property of light can be used – polarisation – something else we cannot see, but some animals can. Many butterflies can discriminate between the angle and strength of polarised light, by comparing how it is detected by different groups of cells in the eye. It is a little bit like how we can tell apart different colours based on cells that respond to certain wavelengths of light. *Heliconius* are not just colourful; many species also have iridescent wings. Iridescence is a phenomenon in which the colour of an object varies with the angle it is seen from. In this case, the scales on a butterfly's wings interfere with light, producing a variety of different colours that depend on the angle from which the butterfly is seen. A feature of iridescent wing colours is that they also reflect markings that differ in their polarisation.

BEHIND THE SCIENCE

Understanding polarised light and how animals see it, can be a real challenge. This is partly because we lack the ability to see it, and polarisation, unlike ultraviolet, is not just an extension of our own colour perception but a different type of vision entirely. Polarised light relates to the way a wave of light travels and oscillates in a certain direction – up and down, side to side and so on, and usually at a specific angle. In most cases, the combined light that reaches us contains a mixture of different polarised light angles, so that we say that the light is, overall, 'unpolarised'. However, as light interacts with and passes through things – particles in the atmosphere or particular surfaces and structures, even polarised sunglasses – it is filtered in such a way that the light is dominated by certain angles of polarisation. Many animal species, ranging from ants and dragonflies to cuttlefish and mantis shrimp, can detect and discriminate between polarisation angles. It is also possible to work out properties such as the proportion of light that is polarised in a certain orientation, and the overall intensity of polarised light. To communicate, some species create body surfaces and other structures that manipulate polarised light and create recognisable patterns of polarisation. When we think of colour in nature, we often consider three properties: hue (such as red or green), how saturated a given colour is (pink versus red, for example) and how bright the surface is (the amount of light reflected). Crudely, we can imagine the ability to see polarised light as potentially allowing animals to perceive a whole set of features in the world, related to the angle, intensity and proportion of polarised light. It means a whole category of vision may exist that is as rich as our sensation of colour.

For any animal that can discriminate polarised light, parts of the *Heliconius* wing can be seen to shine with strongly polarised markings, whereas other areas of the wing are dull, and the intensity depends on the butterfly species and where it lives. Iridescent wing markings are most prominent in *Heliconius* species that live in the deep forest. Such environments are quite dark and lack strong variation in polarisation, and so any signal that is rich in this type of light should stand out clearly, not least as bright flashes when the insect moves its wings. It means that, across all species of butterflies, those that live in deep forest environments are much more likely to have polarised wing patterns than those that live in more open habitats.

The cydno longwing butterfly may not be the most striking *Heliconius* species, appearing to us as largely blue-black with white patterns. However, its wings glow with polarisation that can be seen by other butterflies, and by ourselves if we have special cameras. The markings are important to these insects during courtship and mating. In experiments, it's been found that males are much less likely to approach and attempt to mate with females when the polarisation part of the wing signal is removed, evidence of its importance in courtship and mating in these species.

The flashes of polarisation, however, are not thought to attract unwelcome attention. While some avian predators may detect polarised light, they are not thought to draw on this ability to catch food; any use they have is probably centred on navigation, detecting polarisation patterns from the sun, for example, rather than finding prey. So, just as with ultraviolet, some *Heliconius* know who to mate with by using polarised markings that stand out to them, but which are largely hidden from prying eyes.

***

We have come a long way in our understanding of how colour is used to recognise species, potential mates and individuals; yet, some mysteries remain. The coloration of many animals is far from fixed during the course of their lives. Among the most common changes are those that occur as individuals mature, generally a transition from a dull or camouflage colour in juveniles to gaudy and elaborate patterns that attract a mate in mature animals. Sometimes, however, changes occur the other way round.

Male blue moon butterflies have wing patches that reflect UV light, and the brightness of these patches may be a signal of fitness to females.

Nearly two-thirds of primate species have been reported to change colour as they grow up. Even in humans, hair colour is often different in babies compared to when we get older. In these primate species, it is often the young that are striking and adorned with a pelage that stands out from all else.

The dusky leaf monkey or spectacled langur is found in the Malay Peninsula. Adults are rather interesting-looking creatures in their own right: fluffy with fuzzy grey fur and marked with prominent white rings around the eyes, resembling spectacles. The colour of the fur can vary among subspecies, but the big surprise is the colour of youngsters – a bright vivid orange that stands out from the grey of the adult coats and the dark green forest backdrop.

Many other primates, including other langur species, have brightly coloured babies. Quite why this phenomenon even exists remains rather mysterious, though we are not short of ideas. For instance, the orange coat might help them with camouflage. As counterintuitive as this might appear, many predators lack a visual system that enables them to tell reds and oranges from greens and browns, such that orange might actually blend into the forest in the eyes of aggressors. It is a nice idea, but it's hard to escape the point that simply being dull brown or even grey would afford even more effective concealment. Another suggestion is that the orange stands out to primates who have good colour vision and so stops the babies from being lost or misplaced. Similarly, the orange might act as a symbol that the animals are juveniles, encouraging other females in the group to help care for them. This status symbol might also prevent aggression from potential rivals, since being shown as a juvenile means that the baby should not be thought of as a competitor for partners or rank. The truth is we don't really know the answer. All these factors may play a role, although

Mother and baby dusky leaf monkeys in Thailand. Striking differences in appearance between adults and young are common in primates, yet the reasons are unknown.

many researchers plump for the theory that the coat colour of young primates is a symbol that they are recognised as immature juveniles rather than adults. Whatever the reason, these little characters certainly stand out for the first six months of their lives, gradually turning grey as they grow older.

Coloration in nature has a critical role to play for many animals to clearly identify those with whom they interact. It enables them to recognise species and individuals, and to identify potential partners. In many instances, the signals used are conveyed in colours hidden from the eyes of predators and other threats… and also ourselves. The need to identify one another is also an important driving force leading to some of the great diversity in life observed, both within and among species. Determining who and what an individual is may be one thing, but for many animals to be able to mate, they must also impress potential partners with their vibrant displays and extravagant costumes.

Disparity in costumes between males and females in nature could hardly be better illustrated than by the twelve-wired bird-of-paradise from New Guinea.

CHAPTER TWO

ATTRACTING MATES

Colour patterns can convey a great deal more information than simply recognising a species or an individual. The way an animal looks, especially its colour, can reveal what condition it is in now, or was previously in, how capable it is at finding food, or even how good a father a male might be. In fact, of all the many uses of colour, the need to attract a mate has led to some of the most spectacular displays in the natural world.

Females tend to be the choosy ones, closely inspecting the costumes of males, in order to pick the best of the bunch as a partner and father for their offspring. Males, therefore, are generally the more brightly decorated and expected to dazzle and dance their way to securing a partner. Some mating displays are built in from birth, so a male can perform them as soon as he matures. Others take years of practice. The bright hues and contrasting patterns are not always fixed. Many creatures can manipulate colour and change the way they look. They can even modify the world around them, and so show off their attractiveness to the maximum possible effect.

***

India is home to one of the most familiar and stunning of all birds – the peacock. Many of us know peacocks best from stately homes and parks, but in the wild the peacock must survive in the forest, balancing the need to attract a mate with the importance of not being eaten by the predators that lurk among the trees.

It's no secret that the stunning tail of the peacock is the feature that convinces a peahen he is a worthy partner. It's one of the most impressive sights in nature, a dazzling fan of feathers with up to 150 eyespots, all marked with iridescent blues, greens and purples. Females, though, take some convincing, and courtship takes place at a special rendezvous, known as a lek. Groups of males space themselves out, each with his own little patch where he performs his display. The wider display area, usually some sort of forest clearing, can at times be packed with several peacocks, all trying to win over the females who come to carefully inspect them. Usually, one or two males get the lion's share, while the other males finish the day empty handed.

In the natural world, males tend to be the showy ones, exemplified by the fiery-throated hummingbird.

In the Andaman Sea, a male flame anthias displays to a female.

To our eyes, they are all so overwhelmingly colourful that it can be hard to see how they differ, and what exactly is especially attractive. The point is that not all males look exactly the same – some have more eyespots, others have brighter or more colourful tails, and a few have a more energetic dance. These exuberant males usually win the day and subsequently gain all the mating opportunities.

Charles Darwin once famously said of the peacock's tail that it 'makes me sick'. It wasn't so much the gaudy nature of the plumage that caused him such distress, as the problem it created at the time for his theory of evolution by natural selection. Darwin's great synthesis was based on the survival of the fittest (a term coined not by Darwin, but by English biologist Herbert Spencer), whereby organisms are in a constant battle for existence. How could a bird like a peacock afford such an extravagant tail, when it must surely be a beacon to predators and a major restriction on movement, especially flight? The massive tail of the peacock certainly is a constraint, and it can hardly help the poor bird to move around the cluttered forest environment, where it inevitably uses an enormous amount of energy to avoid obstacles and predators. As it happens, Darwin himself ultimately found the answer – creatures don't merely need to survive, but crucially, they must also reproduce and pass on their characteristics to the next generation.

One of the major battles many animals, particularly males, face is in trying to convince members of the opposite sex that they are a worthy partner. In his theory of sexual selection, Darwin realised that females exert considerable pressure on males to look stunning in order to draw the female's eye. In essence, Darwin suggested that females have aesthetic preferences, and this, over time, has driven the evolution of ever more dramatic and elaborate mating displays.

The striking multi-coloured eyespots on the feathers of male Indian peafowl.

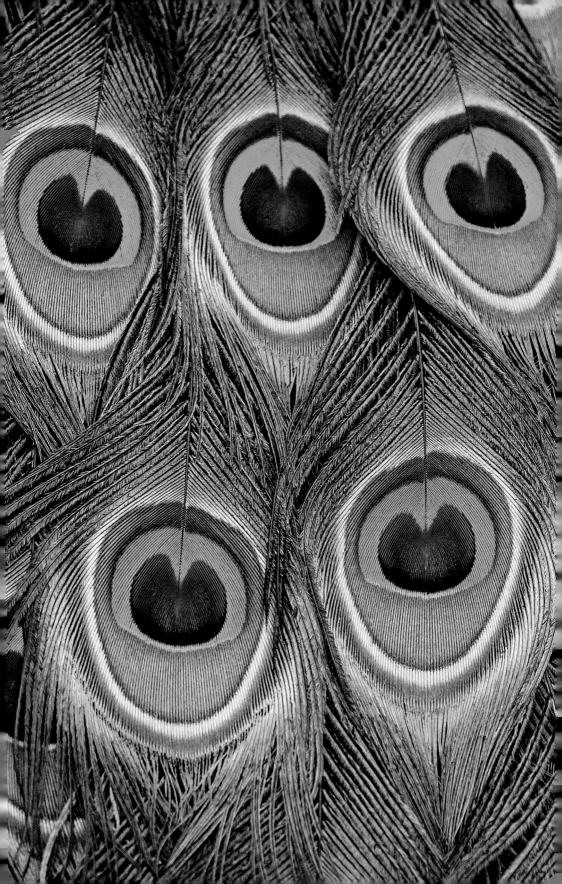

In many ways, Darwin was decades ahead of his time. To a conservative Victorian society, the idea of females holding the cards, when it came to choosing partners, was not well received. As obvious as it seems to us now, it was well into the mid to late twentieth century before people really began to accept that female choice not only existed, but was commonplace. A wealth of scientific research supports this being a major reason for why many male animals look the way they do. They have been placed into a long evolutionary battle to look more and more beautiful to grab the attention of females. What has remained debatable is exactly *why* females should do the choosing in the first place.

A female black grouse turns her back on two males displaying at a lek in Scotland.

BEHIND THE SCIENCE

Female choice has garnered much attention from biologists. While they recognise several reasons why females are picky, there is disagreement about the extent to which these different ideas are correct. While we may not always see the differences ourselves, even animals of the same species and sex vary greatly in their ability to run or fly, find food or resist disease. Evolution is all about passing on your genes, so a diligent parent requires what is the best for its offspring. A mother might, therefore, choose a male based on the direct benefits he can provide – that is, how good he may be at bringing home food or protecting the nest from danger. In doing so, the young should have the best opportunity to survive to adulthood, when they can themselves start to reproduce.

Another idea is that females choose potential fathers based on the quality of their genes: often called 'indirect benefits'. A male, for example, might have a strong immune system, excellent eyesight or great physical strength. By choosing such a partner, there is a good chance that the mother's children will also inherit these traits and benefit from them. In both direct and indirect benefits, the male's mating display should be a reliable indicator of how good he really is. There is, in fact, another large area of science focusing on what prevents inferior males from being able to cheat the system. One explanation is that only the best-quality males can afford to have the most extravagant displays. Given that producing vibrant colours can require a lot of energy, or that having an enormous tail may restrict flight or risk predation, only the fittest males can manage such 'handicaps'. Those that try to cheat are picked off. Alternatively, some ornaments may simply be beyond the reach being made by inferior males – a male of small body size may be constrained by having a similarly small tail, and there's nothing he can do about it.

A further reason why females might choose, rather similar to some of Darwin's own ideas, but developed some years after, is that selecting an attractive partner is in itself valuable. If peahens show preferences for males with, say, lots of brightly coloured eyespots, then by mating with a male with an impressive tail, the female might ensure that her sons share this attribute. In turn, they will be attractive to females themselves when they grow up, and have a better chance of breeding. Through evolution, we can end up with a scenario whereby male sexual signals and female preferences get locked together and, over time, they become ever more extreme, leading to such a stunning display as the peacock's tail. This doesn't tell us why females should have preferences for specific features in the first place, such as favouring red spots or blue stripes, but scientists know that the visual systems of many animals are more strongly stimulated by certain patterns, shapes and colours, and it may be that males evolve features that exploit these pre-existing 'preferences' in the female's sensory system.

Seeing through the cacophony of sights and sounds of a courtship ritual to discover how males differ, let alone pick out the prize specimen, may seem like a challenge to us, yet among all the fervour of the mating display, there is an order to things. Indeed, many females are able to pick out the most desirable male, in spite of the intense competition for their attention. To a large extent, the female must take her time to compare her suitors, whereas each of the males must stand out, hold her gaze and show off the best he has to offer.

On the peacock lek, each male vigorously shakes his tail, shimmering the eyespots and colours, while making a rattling sound. Light is key to his success. The true splendour of his plumage is only revealed in sunlight, and the luckiest (or perhaps most vigorous) male will hold court in the brightest morning sunshine, leaving many of the other males, quite literally, in the shade. Rays of light cause the male's plumage to dazzle and sparkle with iridescence, and he has another trick to enhance this effect – he manoeuvres the female in front of him and holds his plumage at an angle of 45 degrees to the sun, where the light enhances the blues and greens most of all. The eyespots themselves, especially on the lower part of the tail. serve to capture and hold the female's attention. Shaking and rattling the tail reinforces the effect, capturing the female's attention more effectively. The overall size of his tail could also be attractive from afar.

It might seem like a lot of effort for the peahen to be so choosy; after all, most of the males look spectacular. Yet she has good reasons. Not all research completely agrees, but males with the greater number of eyespots are, as we would expect, often more likely to be chosen by females. These males also tend to be in a better condition and healthier generally. Not only that, but females who choose more adorned males as partners tend to have young that survive better when they grow up.

There is another reason why Darwin need not have worried quite so much about the peacock and its conspicuous tail. While the feathers may be the epitome of gaudiness to us, they don't appear that way to many predators. For a large bird, medium-sized and large predatory mammals pose the greatest risk, from big cats, such as leopards and tigers, to smaller mammals, including civets, mongooses and wild dogs. Those carnivores don't see as many colours as we do – or, indeed, the birds

Overleaf: In Bandhavgarh National Park, India, the full splendour of a male Indian peafowl is on show as he attempts to dazzle onlooking females with the extravagance of his tail plumage.

themselves, which have even better colour vision than humans. The eyes of a bird like a peacock contain four types of light-sensitive cells used to see colours. These cones, as they are known, capture light from the very short ultraviolet and violet parts of the spectrum, right up to greens and reds at the other end, enabling the birds to perceive a greater range of colours than we see. Consider how colourful the peacock's tail is to us, and then imagine how it might appear to a peahen that sees the world with even more vibrancy. Mammalian predators, on the other hand, can't tell apart many colours that we would see as greens, yellows and reds, and they also fail to perceive detailed patterns. When scientists have estimated how visible the plumage of a peacock is to their enemies, the answer is that it's not very visible at all – the tail actually blends into the environment quite well. Darwin had no need to feel ill.

* * *

Peacocks may epitomise all that is colourful and extravagant about male mating costumes in nature, but there is another group of creatures, named after their avian counterparts, that can even exceed the bird's colourfulness: peacock spiders. These tiny jumping spiders, just a few millimetres long, have colour patterns and performances that take things to another level.

At a recent count, there were 86 described species, most of them formally identified in the past 10 to 15 years. In fact, there are probably many others out there waiting to be discovered, and they all originate from Australia, particularly the forests and scrublands of Western Australia. It's not hard to see how they got their name – females tend to be dull browns and greys and largely inconspicuous, while males are spectacular. The head and legs are covered with bright hues and patterns, but it is the abdomen that shows off a kaleidoscope of colours – blues, reds, greens, yellows, all in glorious metallic iridescence – and some species even have flaps on the abdomen that they can extend when they display. Much as the peacock bird extends his tail, the spiders wave their abdominal flaps to impress the opposite sex. Each species also has its own colour pattern. In some, the males have bright blue abdomens with red spots and stripes, all outlined in fiery yellow, whereas others have black and white stripy legs that they hold aloft when they display. One species called *Maratus constellatus* is named for its blue abdomen with yellow spots that look like paintings of stars. The most well-

The stellar markings on the back of **Maratus constellatus**
from Western Australia.

known species, *Maratus volans*, has red and grey stripes on the head, and an abdomen marked with two halves of bright yellow, separated by metallic green, blue and red stripes, together with green circles spreading out in lines around the abdominal flap.

With birds, peahens choose male peacocks based on the number and colourfulness of the eyespots on the male's tail, but what about female peacock spiders – what impresses them most? The existence of a handful of peacock spider species has been known since the late 1800s, but because they only really attracted the attention of scientists and naturalists alike in the last decade or so, we actually don't know a huge amount about them. In fact, most species and their behaviour have not been studied at all. Most of what we do understand is from work on *Maratus volans*. This is the poster child of the group and it is certainly extravagant.

Males combine their dazzling coloration and dance moves, during which they wave their legs and abdomens around in front of females, with a series of tactile signals. They tap their legs and other body parts on the ground and vegetation, sending vibration signals to females, while at the same time waving their extravagant abdomens. The vigour of the movement predicts male mating success, and this appears to be more important than the vibration signals. Essentially, the more effort a male puts into his dance moves, and the longer he dances, the more likely he is to succeed. It may be that the vibrations alert and attract female attention, and then the mating dance is ultimately what matters, so why the vibrant colours and patterns?

Peacock spiders, like all jumping spiders, have excellent vision. Their huge (compared to their body) forward-facing eyes see fine detail, and inside their eyes are receptor cells that enable many species to visualise a whole spectrum of colours, including ultraviolet, so a female can clearly see the colour patterns a male

The iconic version of a peacock spider is **Maratus volans.** *The male is extravagantly coloured, yet only 5 millimetres long.*

is showing off. Strangely, however, most studies of peacock spiders have looked primarily at the movement and vibration signals rather than the colours. Nevertheless, such vivid colours are no accident and they clearly play a key role. What little work has been done suggests that longwave colours, such as reds and yellows, are not on their own critical for mating success. It is the contrast between different colour patches that seems to be more important. Females, therefore, may not be judging males based on how red particular patches are, but rather how colourful and striking the ornaments are as a whole. This makes sense, because as the tiny spiders dance around, showing off a great variety of colours and patterns, it's hardly going to be easy for a female to closely inspect the richness of each colour patch. Just imagine trying to assess a scrap of red on the Union Jack flag when someone is waving it frantically in front of you. This might also explain why some spiders have blue abdomens set with yellow 'stars', and other species have elaborate arrangements of yellows, reds and blue stripes – it's the colour contrast and overall gaudiness that matters, not the specific colours. It's likely that the male's costume denotes his species, whereas the vibrancy of his display appeals to females. Beyond that, as to whether males with more colourful and more vigorous displays are also better individuals, have better genes for coping with the environment, or are in better condition, only time and more investigation will tell.

* * *

Almost anything goes when it comes to peacock spider colours, from the bright blue of Maratus elephans *(top) to the eye-popping red on* Maratus nigromaculatus *(bottom).*

Spanning over 3,000 square kilometres and set high in the Andean mountains, the Atacama salt flats make for a dramatic landscape. Like many deserts, the Atacama is a place of extremes, cycling between temperatures of up to 40°C during the day and just a few degrees at night. Water running down from higher ground quickly evaporates under the omnipresent sun, leaving behind the salts it was carrying, to form a crust on the surface of a shallow lake. Conditions on the salt flats may not suit most animals, but they are rich in food, such as algae and shrimp, which are perfect for the large flocks of flamingos that gather in the salty water. The birds sweep their bills from side to side, collecting the food particles. But feeding is not all the birds do; they have also come here to breed.

Like peacock spiders, flamingos dance. Set against the white salt flats, groups of tens or even hundreds of pink-coloured adults, perform a synchronised dance, ruffing up their feathers and strutting back and forth with their heads raised high, all in an attempt to attract a mate for the breeding season. As they dance, the birds size each other up as potential partners, analysing each other's features and observing just how pink their feathers really are.

Along with the peacock, few birds are as iconic as flamingos. Their bright pink plumage and yellow bills are unmistakable. The colour of their feathers is, however, not a given. In fact, it is only possible owing to their unusual diet. Young flamingos are not pink, but grey, and mature birds, which have spent a great deal of time displaying to partners and then raising chicks, also regress to a paler colour. Regular feeding is needed to keep up appearances.

Andean flamingos, like other flamingos, gain their pink colour through their diet. Over time, carotenoid pigments in the shrimp and algae on which they feed turn their feathers pink.

Flamingos can lose their colour when rearing their young. Their crop milk diverts the nutrients to their chicks.

BEHIND THE SCIENCE

Colour in nature is produced by manipulating the way that light behaves and by changing the spectrum of light that reaches the eyes of others. In humans, we see pinks and reds when the spectrum of light is rich in longer wavelengths, and blues when it is made up predominantly of shorter wavelengths. To create specific colours and patterns, the bodies of animals must change the light that hits them to produce the arrays of blues, greens, yellows and other colours that we observe in nature. Broadly speaking, colour can be produced in two ways.

The first is the use of special pigments. These absorb some wavelengths of light, but reflect others, so that the light bouncing off the animal not only produces certain colours, but also alters how light or dark its markings are. Pigments are most often used to make colours such as reds, browns, yellows and oranges. There are several types. Melanin, the same pigment that changes the darkness of human skin, for example, is a key pigment used to make browns and blacks, such as in the feathers of owls or sparrows. Carotenoids, a group with hundreds of different types of pigments, are used to produce the stunning oranges, yellows and reds of birds' beaks and feathers. Carotenoids, with only a few exceptions, cannot be made by the animals themselves, but must be obtained from their diets, either directly from plants or by eating other creatures that have themselves consumed plant material. This means that the carotenoid pigments used to make warm colours are often a limited resource, and only the fittest individuals can gather sufficient amounts of them to look special. There are several others, including the psittacofulvin pigments made only by parrots for their especially gaudy red, yellow and orange colours.

The second way to produce colours is to use special structures. These are made by forming particular microscopic arrangements of materials in the body, sometimes utilising air pockets and spaces, but with very precise arrangements and intervals between the tissue layers. The arrangements scatter some wavelengths, usually the longer ones, such that only some wavelengths of light remain that can be seen by others. Structural colours tend to be responsible for many of the blues, greens and iridescent colours found in the natural world, including the dazzling blue plumage of a kingfisher or the purple bib of a hummingbird. In many cases, animals combine both structural and pigment mechanisms to create the great variety of colours we observe. Some birds even decorate themselves with make-up from the environment, or from body glands, to modify their appearance further, including the yellow coloration of some hornbill beaks and feathers.

Structural mechanisms and pigments in the feathers enable birds like the rufous-backed kingfisher from Borneo to produce a kaleidoscope of colours.

The blue-green algae and the shrimp that flamingos eat are rich in red and yellow carotenoid pigments, and specifically carotene itself (the same pigment found in many of the vegetables we eat). If a bird's diet is rich enough, it can acquire sufficient amounts of these pigments to make its feathers pink and its bills yellow. As the food is digested, the flamingo extracts the pigments and converts them to other forms, before adding them to its feathers. It's rather like dyeing the feathers from the inside out. Naturally, not all food sources are the same, so flamingos living in some parts of the world, such as the Caribbean, are often a deeper pink than birds occurring elsewhere, such as in parts of Kenya. Some species of flamingo, such as the greater flamingos living in the wetlands of southern Spain, can even take the pigments consumed and secrete the key dyes from them through a special preen gland at the base of the tail. They rub these cosmetics directly onto their neck and head and also transfer the dye to their upper back. This is time-consuming, but it makes their plumage even redder in colour. They must keep up this behaviour, however, since birds that stop applying make-up begin to fade in the bright sun after just a few days.

For a young flamingo, it can take up to five years to reach peak pink, and adults will sometimes take two years out from breeding to recover their looks. Flamingos can live beyond 40 years old, so looking after themselves is a vital consideration. Carotenoids have another essential function for many animals in that they also play a vital role in the immune system and in maintaining good health. Carotenoids are even in the visual pigments found in the eyes, so help to maintain effective colour vision. So, there's a trade-off – any pigment used to make the feathers pink is taken away from maintaining good health. The pinkest birds are thought to therefore be those that are strongest, fittest, best at gaining resources like food and helping to raise a healthy chick. Those birds are the ones that get first pick of the mates. Not only that, but more colourful, better fed birds can start to breed earlier and get access to the best nesting sites. After breeding, the birds start to use more of the carotenoid pigments they ingest for other body functions instead, and their coloration begins to fade once more. During breeding, the mothers also pass carotenoids into their eggs, making the yolk bright red, and parents will even feed chicks with a blood-red milk from their beaks. Doing this further drains the pink colour from the adult birds, adding to the time they must take to regain their looks.

***

People often say, 'You are what you eat,' and, for flamingos, it's the very reason that they're pink. The same substance in their diet is sometimes added to sausages to give them more colour.

While some birds, like flamingos, dance in synchrony to show off their colourful plumage, others perform alone, highlighting their scintillating hues in a stunning display of aerobatics. Their movement and performance serve to enhance how effectively a male appeals to onlooking females. In the Sonoran and Mojave deserts and in coastal areas of California lives a tiny bird. Weighing just 2–3 grams and less than 10 centimetres long, the

The male Costa's hummingbird has a purple throat patch that flares out during courtship. The iridescent feathers catch the sunlight to show off his bright colours.

male Costa's hummingbird darts rapidly between flowers in a flash of colour. The female has green plumage on its back, with grey and white underparts, but the male has a striking addition – a deep iridescent purple throat patch that shimmers and changes colour as he moves his head around. For this miniature bird, its colours and movement are key to its success.

Costa's hummingbirds migrate the comparatively short distance (compared to other hummingbirds) northwards from Mexico and arrive in the desert in late winter and early spring to breed, before it gets too hot. Males then defend territories, where they drink nectar from a range of flowers, eat insects on the wing and, crucially, attract females. The wide open spaces should allow for good visibility, not least as males sit high up on perches to ward off rivals, but males are so small that they would be easy to miss. To compensate, and to show off his dazzling colours, each male performs a spectacular flight display. Rising 10 metres into the air, he then closes his wings and nosedives, before rising rapidly up again in a U-shaped flight. As he dives, wind rushes through his tail feathers, producing a loud whistle as he travels. He also performs a so-called 'shuttle display', where he swings from side to side and fans out his neck feathers so that his iridescent plumage sparkles. The changes in direction serve to further show off the shimmering colours from purples to pinks, especially as they catch the bright sunlight. His entire display is intended to woo discerning females. While successful males may breed with several partners in the season, each female mates just once and she must then expend much time and effort incubating the eggs and raising her chicks – she needs to make the right choice, and the male's job is to convince her that he is the one.

***

Iridescent plumage is a trick that many birds use. It involves manipulating light so that it takes on a different hue, depending on the angle from which the display is seen. More specialist and rare, however, is a manipulation of light that is so extreme it can make the colours of mating signals appear to glow. In the forests of far northeast Australia, the male Victoria's riflebird moves between shafts of dappled light in small clearings on the forest floor. He calls out to attract a female. She is dull brown, well camouflaged, and arrives on a nearby branch waiting for his performance to begin. The male then ruffles his feathers, raises his wings in a curve around his body and shows off his plumage. As he displays, he mechanically moves his body from side to side,

Striking a pose, a male Victoria's riflebird from Queensland, Australia, hopes to attract a female.

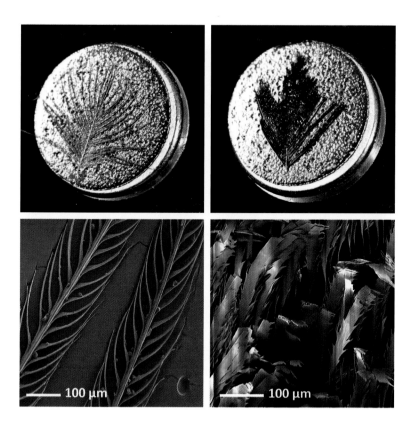

showing off his black feathers and the metallic blue plumage on his chest, throat and crown. The female joins in and eventually they mate. The male's dance is something he was able to do from birth, yet it needed perfecting over a period of years by practising with groups of other males. His moves, however, would be of little use were it not for his striking colours.

Birds like the Victoria's riflebird and a variety of bird-of-paradise species found in New Guinea are also known to have feathers that are blacker than black and, rather than shining, are seemingly matte in appearance. Their feathers are not merely dark, like those of a blackbird, but so dark that they almost look

Normal black and super-black feathers (above), and barbules on black and super-black feathers (below).

like holes without any light at all. These types of markings in nature are called 'super-black'. Using special technology, scientists can measure just how much light they absorb, and it turns out that the feathers of these birds absorb as much as 99.5 per cent of all the light that hits them. How they do this comes down to the structure of the feathers. On normal black feathers, the minute filaments called barbules lie mostly flat, allowing some light to bounce back rather than be absorbed. Super-black feathers, however, have barbules that stick up and curve, like a boomerang, so they repeatedly trap the light as it bounces around within the feather, until sooner or later it is absorbed. The feather structures are also directional – the effect of the blackness is greater when viewed from a position that a female would normally observe a male mating display.

The question is why birds-of-paradise might use super-black. The birds are rarely black all over and are usually adorned in a variety of stunning colours, such as vibrant blues, reds, yellows and iridescent greens. It is well known that the perception of any given colour depends on the context under which it is seen. A major influencing factor is the other colours that surround it. A given colour looks less vivid, for example, if surrounded by lots of other bright colours. To make it stand out, these birds-of-paradise, as well as some species of butterflies, will pair vivid hues alongside or set into a super-black background. The effect is to make the colours appear more vivid and even glow against the blackness that surrounds them. The superb bird-of-paradise, one of the species most revered for the male's incredible mating display, illustrates this better than any other species. When trying to impress a female, the male throws his black wing cape into an arc as he displays, so that his electric blue chest and eye patches seem to almost float in the air and glow in front of her eyes. It's almost psychedelic and certainly hypnotic.

Rich blue set against super-black makes for a striking decoration in the growling riflebird from Papua New Guinea.

BEHIND THE SCIENCE

Birds evolved from a group of theropod dinosaurs, which includes iconic predators, such as *Tyrannosaurus rex*. Time and again people have speculated on what the headline-grabbing ancestors of birds would have looked like. Remarkably, discoveries and advances in recent years have opened up the possibility of revealing the actual appearances of these and other extinct animals. For decades, reconstructions of dinosaur colours have been based on intuition. If we know the sort of habitat that a dinosaur lived in, and features such as its size and how it lived its life, then we can deduce how it might have appeared – whether, for example, it had brown-green camouflage patterns to blend in among trees. Add to that any obvious features, such as the back plates of *Stegosaurus*, and a hopefully not inaccurate reconstruction of the animal can be made. Unfortunately, the actual colours, how bright the animal was, what patterns it had and where they were placed were essentially guesswork. Yet recent fossil discoveries, especially those where the soft tissues of dinosaurs have been rapidly preserved before decaying, coupled with advanced imaging and high-powered microscopes, enable more precise reconstructions.

Some of the most important discoveries showed that many dinosaurs were covered with feathers, completely changing our view of how these ancient reptiles appeared. In some species, the feathers were relatively well developed. This included a dinosaur called *Microraptor*, found in China and dating back 120 million years. It had wings on its legs and arms, perhaps used in gliding. Other dinosaurs, including even *T. rex*, may have been covered in downy feathers. Feathers did not evolve in the first instance for flight, but instead probably for insulation, and quite likely they were also used in display. Far from the uniform scaly skin depicted in most books, some dinosaurs were feathered, fluffy and ornamented. Even more crucially, preserved in the fossils of some dinosaurs are the remains of minute organelles that hold melanin, and the structural arrangement of them. Careful analyses by scientists can reveal the colours that these arrangements might have produced and, if enough of the body is preserved, the markings that they would have made. The science is not without controversy, but it means we now know that, for example, some dinosaurs were probably made of dark and light patterns, like a magpie, or had a red-brown head crest. Fossils of *Microraptor* suggest that it had structural layers of melanin pigments that would have given rise to black feathers with iridescent blues. Rather like a starling, the colour of its plumage likely changed with the lighting, and this was perhaps valuable in attracting a mate. *Microraptor* also had relatively long and wide tail plumage, something that may have also been used in courtship displays. *Velociraptor*, made infamous in films such as *Jurassic Park*, though in reality much smaller, was likely covered in fluffy feathers, except on its tail and arms (wings). It probably didn't fly, so the longer feathers on the body extremities hint at colourful plumage being used in communication, and perhaps to shield its nest. Knowing what behaviour accompanied the dinosaurs' costumes is harder to deduce, but evidence of scrapes in the ground from dinosaurs living in the Cretaceous period has led some scientists to speculate that these were mating leks, akin to those of the peacock. Fossils of other, larger, herbivorous dinosaurs have shown them to use types of camouflage patterning.

At present, because melanin gives rise to blacks and browns, until we can find evidence of other colour pigments in dinosaur fossils we can't know their true colours, or whether they were as extravagantly coloured as some birds or lizards, but we are getting closer. Indeed, carotenoids have been found preserved in the fossils of 10-million-year-old snakes. In time we may know even more about what the mating displays of these long-extinct animals truly looked like.

In the streams of Trinidad lives a fish familiar to many aquarium hobbyists – the guppy. Enter almost any pet shop and there will be a tank of these small fish, each a few centimetres long, displaying their bright oranges, reds and iridescent blues. For so long have guppies been an aquarium staple that many captive-bred varieties exist, all bolder and brighter than their wild relatives. Individuals living in the freshwater streams around Central and South America are, nonetheless, still beautiful, magnificently marked with colours and patterns that vary from one individual to the next; few males look the same. The splendour of their colours is enhanced by the guppies' shoaling behaviour. As is often the case, the females are much duller than the males.

Beyond its value as a pet, the guppy is one of the animals that has been most widely studied by biologists for its use of colour and vision. Guppies eat a variety of foods, from fruits to insects, but one important aspect of their diet is to obtain carotenoids. These are important not only for their health, but also for display at breeding time.

The situation varies between guppy populations, but many females have a particular affinity for orange. The attraction seems to be linked with the guppy's visual system being tuned to detect the orange colours of its food. Beyond orange, guppies have excellent colour vision generally. In experiments, those fish raised on foods rich in carotenoids have a visual system better at seeing oranges and reds than fish fed on diets where the pigments were more limited. In guppies, vision, diet, health and colour are, therefore, all linked. In courtship, male colour provides important information: males with brighter orange spots may be those that are in better health, more adept at foraging, carrying fewer parasites and in general better at survival. Competition is often fierce, so much so that males have some surprisingly clever tactics to get one over on their rivals.

A female (top) and a series of male guppies, showing their colour variation.

Like the birds-of-paradise using super-black, the impact of colour patches displayed on these fish depends on what surrounds them; colours look brighter when surrounded by dull patterns. Male guppies use this to their advantage. Some individuals associate in groups with males that have duller colour patches so that their own patterns look gaudier than they really are. Males will also display at times of day when the light conditions best show off certain hues.

In a world where all that matters is securing a mate, guppy colour is brighter, with increasingly more elaborate spots of blues and oranges over the body and fins. The problem for these small fish, though, is that they also make a good bite-sized meal for predators, such as cichlids and killifish. These hunters are adept at targeting prey using vision, and the bright colours of guppies do not only make them stand out to mates and rivals, but also to those bent on eating them. Evolution has an answer, however, with a trade-off between breeding and staying alive. In Trinidadian streams, where predators are absent or rare, male colours are unconstrained by the risk of being detected and so have become extremely colourful. By contrast, in waterways where predators lurk around every corner, the males are much duller.

The evolution of differences in the appearance of male guppies has happened over many generations. Those males that are attractive to females, while at the same time avoiding being eaten, are those that sire more offspring. Over time, the balance of colour between successful courtship and avoiding predation spreads through the local population, as the generations move on. Some animals, though, are more flexible. They can find the ideal balance within their own lifetime by dramatically changing colour. While many birds use high-speed flight, dance moves and iridescent or super-black plumage to show off the glory of their mating signals, a surprisingly large number of animals are capable of going much

Male Indian bullfrogs congregate during the rains,
transforming from camouflage to a vibrant yellow and
contrasting deep blue vocal sacs.

further and fundamentally altering their appearance over time. As with the guppies, in many cases the need for colour change comes from the importance of balancing the benefits of being seen by those whom you want to impress, versus not attracting unwanted attention from animals that might do you harm.

* * *

In the midst of the monsoon season across the Indian subcontinent, groups of very large frogs gather in temporary pools of water. They're Indian bullfrogs, up to 16 centimetres long and a standard green and brown, so not especially remarkable, except for their size in comparison to other local frogs. During the breeding season, however, the males undergo a stunning transformation.

Overnight, they morph from a dull camouflage to something much more extravagant, as their bodies take on a garish yellow hue, and their vocal sacs a bright blue colour.

Normally, the frogs are active mostly at night, but during the rains they become more active in the early daytime too, when individuals search out pools in which to congregate and convince females to mate with them. Males jostle and fight for position, hoping to attract the attention of the females, which remain the standard dull colour and float just below the water surface with their eyes sticking out to watch for prospective partners. The bright yellow of the males stands out against the murky water, but the use of blue makes for an even more dramatic display. These frogs can see the contrast between yellow and blue, one of the most ancient forms of colour vision in nature. As each male calls, its blue sacs inflate and deflate, creating a stunning moving pattern set against the frog's yellow body. The combination of bright colours and the mating call helps females recognise potential mates, and helps males to identify rivals. Once females have chosen a mate, the pair head off somewhere a little quieter away from the mêlée to lay the eggs, and, when all is done, the male frogs start to change back. Within a few days, they return to their camouflaged uniform.

Colour change in these animals enables them to blend in or stand out from their surroundings when they need to, and to not pay the costs of being the wrong colour had their appearance been fixed. A few animals, most notably cuttlefish and octopus, can change rapidly, within seconds. For most creatures, however, the change is slower, taking hours or days. This can enable them to blend in with the changing seasons, like a white snowshoe hare in winter, or to adjust their appearances as they move from one environment to another. In the case of the male bullfrogs, colour change lets them stand out and show off their stunning breeding costumes, but to do so only temporarily so that the heightened risk of being seen by predators is for as short a period as possible. For the rest of the year they can rely on camouflage to blend into their surroundings.

***

Merging with the environment for much of the year is not the top priority for black-and-white snub-nosed monkeys. These endangered primates live only in the forests of the southern Chinese province of Yunnan, at high altitudes of over 3,000 metres, coping with freezing conditions while feeding on lichen. They have a comical appearance, with fluffy grey-brown pelage, dark eyes, a pushed-up nose and a pale white or pink face mask. Although the nose may give them their name, the other key feature is their plump red lips.

Their social life is important, as it is for most primates. In snub-nosed monkeys, a select few older males are the ones that hold family groups and mate with the females. These groups comprise one male, plus three to five females and any young. Other family groups live nearby, but each tends to keep some distance to reduce aggression between the males. Other males, often those that are immature or younger, tend to live in bachelor groups that stay close by. At times, the different groups come closer together to make up larger bands, with several hundred individuals, and within these groups males sometimes come into conflict, so there needs to be a way of communicating, and the lips play an important role.

In males, the lips become redder as they get older, and the colour is more intense during the breeding season (August and September). The reason is not fully understood, but it's possible that the reddening is something preferred by females; essentially,

females find males more attractive when males have redder lips. As males come into breeding age and good condition, and begin to hold groups, the red colour shows them off as a suitable mate, and, once the breeding season commences, male lips redden further in order to make the male even more attractive. This change may be a symbol that the male is the best and strongest individual around, both to mate with and to take charge of the group. As it happens, the lips of males that don't hold dominant positions actually lighten during the breeding season. The reason for this may be that, by making their lips less red, those monkeys are signalling their subordinate status and reducing the likelihood of coming into conflict with a dominant male. It's not clear which of these possibilities – male competition and a signal of social rank or female mate choice – is the main driver of lip colour, but it certainly seems to relate to mating, and there's little doubt that it is a striking feature of these bizarre animals.

The colour of a male, and the spectrum of light that a female can see, are clearly of great importance in mating; yet there is more to successful mating than this. Standing out in the environment is crucial, and behaviour can be key. This is not just in the synchronised movements that a male makes, but also in how he enhances the beauty of his coloration. A green bird choosing to display against a forest backdrop might blend in rather than stand out. He would do much better by performing his dance set against a wide expanse of blue sky. But animals do more than just choose where they court females – some have neat tricks to modify their local environment and make their colours stand out, or even take the role of architect and construct features that draw females in.

A female Yunnan snub-nosed monkey, with baby, from China. The red lips probably convey information on status and breeding potential.

The prize for the most spectacular of all mating costumes must belong to the birds-of-paradise, and a strong contender for the overall crown is the magnificent bird-of-paradise. Found in the tropical rainforests of New Guinea, this bird exemplifies how to stand out and show off with colours. The dense forest environment is relatively gloomy, so male birds-of-paradise must search for suitable clearings to display in. Like some other birds, however, the males don't just accept the current conditions; they modify them to best show off their colours. Each male clears away unwanted debris from his chosen 'court', things that might downgrade the splendour of his plumage or distract a female's attention. He also looks for vertical perches, upright branches or saplings, onto which he hops to show off, not just to one, but often to several females that have come to judge him, alongside immature males that have come to learn from his performance.

The male magnificent bird-of-paradise uses a sapling as a dance pole to show off his colourful plumage.

A crescendo is reached when the male expands his breast shield, seen here from the side (top); but, from the female's vantage point, the magnificent iridescent green plumage is clear to see.

He is quite something to behold – two shining blue-green wire-like tail feathers curl out from his behind, rich yellow wings and electric blue legs, with an iridescent green shield spread out and a red-brown head crown. The waiting females must take it in turns to watch his display from a prime position and then decide if he is good enough or whether to head elsewhere.

While birds like the magnificent bird-of-paradise modify a display court in order to appear their best to females, some take this behaviour much further. In the eastern regions of Australia lives a bird that uses bright colours to stand out. While attractive in his own right, the male enhances not his own plumage, but something he builds. This is the satin bowerbird. Males take five to seven years to develop their mature plumage colours, and it is worth the wait: glossy blue-black feathers, a yellow beak and beautiful eyes with a purple iris mark them out from the olive-green colours of females and immature males. The adult male, however, is not done. During the mating season, much like other bowerbirds, he builds a special structure, the bower. This is not a nest – he takes no part in raising the chicks – but rather an arena in which to display to females. It is made of two sides of vertically arranged twigs and branches, decorated with things the bird has collected. When looking to mate, females will visit the bowers of males, whereby the male is set into action performing a mating dance to the female, strutting around, raising his wings and calling out. If the female is impressed, she'll accept him and mate.

Satin bowerbirds are famous for the things that they add to their bowers. Under natural conditions, away from humans, they add blue feathers, flowers and snail shells. Close to habitation, they are well known to make use of various discarded objects, such as straws, blue bottle tops, ballpoint pens, blue clothes pegs and even shotgun cartridges – anything, in fact, as long as it's

In a Queensland forest, a male satin bowerbird entices females with the blue objects he's collected.

blue. Females clearly like blue, since this is certainly the preferred colour to adorn the bower. When displaying, the male will also often hold one of the coloured objects in his beak.

The females are unquestionably choosy. When building their nests and preparing to breed, they make several visits to a male's bower, and those of rival males, at various stages of its construction. The result is a fierce competition among males to have the best displays and bower decorations, the chances of a mating being higher for those males that perform better displays and have more elaborately decorated bowers. The male, in fact, doesn't always play fair – he has been known to steal the blue decorations from the neighbouring bowers of his rivals, and so scupper their chances while enhancing his own potential success.

The male of another species, the great bowerbird, also manipulates the females' sense of aesthetics to improve his mating

chances, but not by using colour alone; rather, by altering the size of the objects he places around his bower. Great bowerbirds tend to lack the bright decorations used by satin bowerbirds; instead, they build a bower with the two walls of upright twigs and an arena comprising areas that are appropriately called 'avenues'. These avenues are covered with grey and white objects that the male selects, typically bones, pebbles and shells. It is not the decorations themselves that are most important, though, but how they are arranged.

When she visits, the female bowerbird stands at one end of the bower and looks along the avenue in which the male has arranged his decorations. The male performs at the other end. The male knows precisely where the female will stand and where he will display to her, and so arranges the objects with the smallest ones close to where she is standing, and the largest objects furthest away from her. Had he arranged the objects randomly, then the pieces further away from her would have looked smaller and the avenue longer. Instead, by arranging them in a size gradient he creates an illusion called 'forced perspective', which cancels out the perception of size with distance. With this arrangement, the objects on the avenue all look the same size, the avenue itself looks shorter and the male looks bigger. Add to this, he often picks up a colourful object to display with, which contrasts nicely with the dull grey background, and by doing so he can enhance the effect of his mating display. This manipulation of the senses works, since males that build more carefully made size gradients and effective illusions are more likely to be the ones that win over the females.

* * *

A female great bowerbird inspects a male at his bower. She judges his potential as a mate from the arena he's made and his efforts to display.

A bright red bird, marked with purple and blue colours, sits at the entrance to a hole in a tree. It's a parrot, and one of the most breath-taking species. Sitting close by is another bird: vivid emerald green, with a marked orange and yellow beak. The first European naturalists to see these birds thought they were a separate species, so striking is the difference between them, but they are, in fact, both eclectus parrots. The natural world does not generally do hard rules; instead, those that seem to exist are there for breaking. In eclectus parrots, a naïve observer would be forgiven for thinking that the red bird was the male, given that males in nature normally tend to be the showy ones, and females tend to have camouflage plumage. For this species, however, it's the other way round – the red bird is the female.

Opposites attract in eclectus parrots, with a green male courting a red female in the rainforests of northern Queensland.

Eclectus parrots live in the Solomon Islands, New Guinea and northern Australia, nesting high up in the holes of large rainforest trees. That females are the more colourful sex is unusual in nature, and for eclectus parrots the reasons appear to be related to their breeding requirements. In the small number of cases in which female birds are the ones that must compete with one another for males, who are in turn choosy, it is nearly always the case that the male incubates the eggs and cares for the young. Males, therefore, are the ones in demand, often because they hold a valuable resource, such as a nesting site, which may be in short supply. It's a classic case of sex role reversal.

In most avian species, however, the males must compete for females for the opportunity to breed. Females can only produce a

A female eclectus parrot sits in the nest, while a male visits after foraging in the forest.

few eggs per year, whereas males can produce thousands of sperm, which means that females are much more limited in potential numbers of offspring that they can produce than males are. For the female, quality over quantity is key. For the male, mating with an 'inferior' female is inconsequential if he can go off and mate with a series of other females afterwards; that is, of course, assuming he is one of the lucky males that the females like.

Eclectus parrots were for a long time a puzzle, since they do not have sex role reversal. Females are still the limiting factor, and they are the ones that look after the eggs, as with most birds. The reasons for the extreme dimorphism in these birds must be the result of something else, and that is very large differences in the selection pressures that each sex faces.

Holes in trees suitable for nesting are scarce, and mothers must defend them from other females that might try to usurp one and indeed kill her chicks. A female who has a hole will defend it aggressively and spend up to 11 months of the year close by or sitting in the entrance. Fighting females have been known to kill each other over nest sites, and even female parrots of other species need to be driven off. In the build-up to egg-laying, a female will sit in the trees above the hollow, showing off her striking red plumage against the green leaves, advertising to other females that the nest is taken and that it won't be given up without a fight. Birds have excellent colour vision, and red against green offers very high contrast. They are still easy to see with their bright plumage even when sitting in the nest entrance, so they can afford to be more colourful than males, because females can dive into the safety of the nest when threatened by a predator.

Males have no such luxury. Each mother relies on up to five males, with which she breeds, to bring her food. They travel great distances and for several hours each day forage for items, such as fruits, to feed the female and chicks. Males are better off, therefore, being green, albeit a bright green, to be better camouflaged while out foraging. Their green feathers are relatively inconspicuous against the leafy green backgrounds of the forest. By contrast, males are extremely visible when seen against the brown tree trunks, and this matters, because in this location they compete with one another for access and mating opportunities with the females. Although each mother needs many males to help her raise the young, each male would much rather be the one to sire most of the offspring. There is little benefit in having too much competition around. So, in these birds, striking differences in the pressures faced by males and females, and the visual background against which they are seen, have led to some of the most dramatic and unexpected differences in coloration between the sexes observed in nature. It's a lesson in that, to understand why animals look the way they do, we must know about their ecology.

* * *

Bright colours in nature are frequently used to attract partners. Those potential suitors, usually but not always females, tend to be discriminating and on the lookout for mates with the best genes, in the optimal health, and that might make the best fathers. Being gaudy is not without risk and, while animals have a variety of tricks to showcase their extravagant mating ornaments, they often have ways of avoiding being seen when needed, or at least they balance the benefits of mating with the risk of being eaten. Yet, being brightly coloured is not always about convincing choosy partners – sometimes it is as much about fending off rivals and maintaining dominance.

CHAPTER THREE

DOMINANCE & RIVALRY

The huge antlers of a red deer stag or the blubbery bulk of a bull elephant seal, his eyes bulging, as he hammers his teeth into his opponent, are the kinds of images we might have of male animals fighting in the natural world. Colour, we might think, is more for gentle things, such as enticing females, but this assumption can be wrong. Some males are showy and vibrant to display their dominance.

These colourful decorations are of critical importance to reinforce the status of an individual, fend off rivals who may steal access to females, monopolise valuable territories containing resources, such as nesting sites and food, and convey much about an animal's temperament. Colour has even played an important role in the way animals have evolved in their respective environments. Colour can indicate power.

***

The Namibian savannah can be harsh and unforgiving. While wonderfully well adapted, even something as large and imposing as a fully grown giraffe must locate sufficient food and water, stay cool and avoid being eaten by predators. The male of the species must also find a mate. Giraffes are relatively social animals, existing in herds of around 20 females and juveniles, along with a few males, so group dynamics, dominance and colour patterns play important roles in an individual's behaviour and opportunity to procreate. Aside from their exceptionally long necks, one of the most obvious features of these creatures is their markings. A patchwork of white, brown and dark hues looks almost like a jigsaw puzzle, and the pattern varies with species. While species recognition may be one function, there are a number of others, and they depend on the intensity of the colours in the giraffe's coat.

It was once thought that the darkness of a male's markings was simply a sign of his age. The patches do vary from a pale sandy yellow to a deep chocolate brown, and there's no doubt that younger giraffes tend to be lighter, but there is more to it than this. For a start, not all males get darker with age, and some darken less as they mature. Some males even get lighter as they grow older. The variations appear to be linked to an individual's

Battles between male giraffes are a brutal way to assert dominance and breeding rights, like this pair in the Maasai Mara National Reserve, Kenya.

level of dominance. Those with darker spots are more powerful in competitions with rivals. They also tend to be more solitary, moving between groups, while looking for females with which to mate.

The alternative approach is to be a male that hangs out with females and the rest of the group. These males are lighter, less dominant and not strong enough to defend females from rivals. They might be able to obtain some sneaky mating opportunities, though, when dominant males are not around. Lighter-coloured young males may delay mating until they're bigger and stronger, while, at the same time, taking advantage of any chance encounters that come their way. There's little point in fighting, though, when you're too small and immature.

The deeper colour of darker males signals higher testosterone levels and fighting ability and might also indicate that they are better able to withstand intense heat and are generally in good condition. The cost to these males is that they must roam around seeking out groups of females and risk getting into fights with other dominant males.

Thermal imaging of a giraffe herd in Kenya at night shows the heat radiating from their bodies.

The contest follows a set pattern. When two rivals first meet, they size up each other, jostling for position and, using moderate force, they bump their necks together and against one another's body. Normally, this is where it ends, with the more dominant, darker, male maintaining his access to the herd of females, but when two males are evenly matched, things can turn nasty. The giraffes escalate the conflict, using their necks to smash into their opponent's legs and torso, this time with considerable force. The blows can cause serious injury and even knock fully grown giraffes to the ground. Eventually, the stronger male prevails, although he might have to contend with serious injuries too.

As we might also expect, the giraffe's costume appears to play a role in camouflage, breaking up the outline of the body against the savannah vegetation. Giraffes are not often attacked by lions – they have a strong kick and can run surprisingly fast – but it's better not to tempt fate. The markings have another function too – below them lies a network of blood vessels close to the skin's surface, which helps to cool down the animal. The patches themselves radiate heat, keeping the huge animal within its thermal limits, something that can be seen when we look at giraffes with special thermal imaging cameras. Of course, the cost of being darker is that the patches also absorb more heat so, for darker males, life is especially tough: lonely, hot and always at risk of conflict.

The giraffe is one of many mammals for which social status is communicated by appearance, and few animals conjure up such a strong image of power as the giraffe's adversary – the African lion. The male, with his impressive mane of long, dark fur, is often said to be the 'king of beasts', and the mane is what helps successful lions to stay on top of the competition.

Life for a lion is certainly complex and, in a way, political, for success hinges on a balance between friends and enemies. A pride of lions may number just a handful of individuals, or, in some prides, well over 15. As the cubs grow up and mature, the females remain in the group, while the males are ousted and must go it alone or, if they're lucky, with a small team of other males, as many as a half a dozen in some cases. When they are old and strong enough, the mature males can have thoughts of leading a pride, but this is not a given. They must first turf out the current pride leaders, before taking over a pride of their own.

Takeovers are brutal – not only are the current males forced out, but the new males kill all the cubs in the pride. This brings the females into oestrus sooner, so that they can conceive the new males' offspring without any delay. Harsh as it may seem, it also doesn't pay the new pride holders to help raise cubs to which they are unrelated. If the pride is run by a coalition, then the males have to compete for access to females, when an alpha male, quite literally, takes the lion's share, followed by others in order of dominance. Often as not, the males are related, and so they still pass on some of their genes by helping their relatives to breed. The question of course is how males signal their dominance. These animals are powerful and well equipped with weapons that could kill or maim, so it's much safer to signal strength with show instead.

The fact that lion manes differ in appearance is no coincidence, although, unlike many animals, lions do not have excellent colour vision. They see colour, but only as shades of blue and yellow. It would be pointless trying to communicate with red, but they can see clearly differences in light and shade. As a male reaches

Strength and dominance can be signalled by lions with the darkness of the mane.

puberty, his mane begins to darken, a process that continues into adulthood. Those males with darker, hairier manes are individuals that have more testosterone and fighting strength and are in better condition. These lions get more mating opportunities and first access to food at kills and are more likely to be successful in taking over a pride. They also hold the pride and breed for longer, and their offspring have a greater chance of survival. There is a price that these males must pay, however, and that is heat retention. Rather like the giraffes, darker and longer-haired males absorb and retain more heat, which can be a major drawback in some of the hot and dry regions of Africa; in fact, irrespective of dominance, manes tend to be lighter and shorter in hotter areas, and when the season is warmer.

* * *

Some creatures communicate power by using much more vivid displays. The bearded vulture, living in mountain areas in Africa, Asia and Europe, is a large bird, with a wingspan of 2.5 metres or more, and the adults have striking orange or even red feathers on their underparts, neck and head. It's thought that this serves as a symbol of dominance; importantly, as bearded vultures are scavengers, it helps to determine which individual has primary access to the bones on a carcass, for bearded vultures have little interest in meat, only the marrow from bones, which they drop from a height to break them open, so being the dominant bird is crucial for access to such an unpredictable food source.

The birds are not born like this and young birds lack the colourful plumage. Over time, individuals seek out and adorn themselves with mud and soil that is rich in orange iron oxide. Their feathers become stained, and repeated applications of the make-up help to maintain appearances. Not everyone, however,

In the Spanish Pyrenees, a bearded vulture, with neck feathers streaked with red mud, feasts on animal bones.

subscribes to the notion that this behaviour is cosmetic and simply for display. An alternative explanation is that the colouring kills off harmful bacteria that may be living in the feathers. Nevertheless, it's generally thought that, should fights break out, those birds with the brightest orange get first access to food. Older and bigger individuals have a greater intensity of orange and red, and those birds probably hold larger territories and have the time and knowledge to seek out the best sources of soil in which to bathe.

Bearded vultures are not alone in using cosmetics. Birds from hornbills to flamingos enhance their coloration with dyes produced from special glands, but bearded vultures must search out special baths in the habitat. As a consequence, the vultures must work harder to adorn themselves, and this access to key resources may, in itself, be a status symbol.

* * *

West Africa is home to arguably the most colourful of all mammals: the mandrill. It has all the flamboyance of a bearded vulture but, rather than tapping into the environment, it manipulates its appearance more directly. It has excellent colour vision, and it puts on a colourful show of power. Mandrills are imposing primates, by any stretch of the imagination, but to make any impact in their gloomy tropical forest home, bathed in dappled light with a backdrop of green and brown vegetation, they need to use colours that contrast with their environment, and, for this, red and blue is perfect.

It's hard to miss the male. He's three times the size of the females, and a mature individual has colours that look like they have been painted onto his body: a long bright red nose with patches of blue each side and a rump glowing in blue with a

In the gloom of a Gabon forest, colour is power for male mandrills.

short red tail. Charles Darwin, when writing on the evolution of humans, noted how colourful mandrills are compared to most other mammals.

Mandrills are not only the largest of all monkeys, but they also live together in sizable groups. Typically, a single troop includes a dominant male and a dozen or so females, plus immature monkeys of both sexes. When males mature, they leave the group and head off, normally to live a mainly solitary life. Only when they reach breeding age, sometimes at almost ten years old, can they latch on to a troop and compete for mating opportunities. At times, troops come together and live in huge gatherings, called hordes. There might be several hundred monkeys in a horde; in exceptional cases, these have even been said to number more than a thousand. Hordes, inevitably, bring a handful of mature males into proximity with one another, so in smaller groups and even more so in a horde, a male must prove himself to the competition and establish his dominance over rivals in order to lead his troop and have access to females.

Standing out in the forest is one thing, but it's the colour of the nose and rump that conveys information about a male's status. Those with redder noses have more testosterone. They're the strongest, most powerful and most dominant males, as well as being those that have triumphed in recent contests. When an animal loses, or runs away before a fight, the splendour of his red diminishes, although the blue colour flanking the red does not change very much. Blue and red make for a strong visual contrast, however; that's if you can see these hues, and mandrills can.

For a male mandrill, the vividness of the red is crucial, especially when set against blue, to signal both his dominance and how attractive he is to females, while standing out effectively in his forest environment. Fights are not especially common. When they do occur, the physical violence can be serious. On rare occasions, the loser is killed. It's clearly much better to avoid this and instead rely on gestures such as teeth grinding and head bobbing, and on colour to decide who would be the victor. Under most circumstances, two males will tend to be mismatched – one will clearly be weaker, smaller or in worse condition – and, by communicating this with colour, the rivals avoid wasting time reaffirming this physically. Fights tend to break out only when two males are evenly matched, and neither is willing to back down. Even then, one male mandrill will often pull out and show his submission – with a turn and presentation of a blue bottom to the victor. Eventually, however, the time of any male comes to an end, and he will either relinquish his position voluntarily, or be vanquished with force.

As they mature, male mandrills develop a colourful mask and bright rump, which act to communicate dominance.

BEHIND THE SCIENCE

Mandrills are old-world monkeys, and these primates – along with the great apes such as chimpanzees, bonobos and gorillas, as well as us – have evolved excellent colour vision, but we all did so in a rather roundabout way. Long ago in the evolutionary past, the creatures that were the ancestors of modern fish, amphibians, reptiles and birds had been lucky enough to possess excellent colour vision; better than that of humans, in fact. These animals, and many of their modern-day descendants, see colour in the world by using four types of light-sensitive cone cells in the eye, detecting light ranging from ultraviolet through blue, green and red. Having a visual system with four different types of cone, which can see light widely across the spectrum, often equates to excellent colour perception. A person with normal colour vision, who is not colour blind in any way, sees colour with three cone types.

Good colour vision does not come free, however. For the eye to fit in all these cone types, it has to limit the number of other cells it can use. That means, for example, fewer rod cells for seeing effectively in the dark. Somewhere in the evolutionary history of mammals, perhaps thanks to being pushed aside by the dominant dinosaurs, our mammalian ancestors became progressively more nocturnal and active in darker, more secluded places. In the gloom, colour vision is less useful; instead, the premium is on seeing brightness and contrast. As such, evolution favoured those animals that gave up some of their cones in order to improve their brightness and night vision. Most mammals bear that burden to this day, seeing the world with just two cones and perceiving shades of colour that we would see as blues and yellows. Some went even further, with many marine mammals giving up colour vision entirely.

At some point, after the dinosaurs had had their time, groups of mammals became more active during the day again and adopted ways of life where better colour vision is valuable. For one thing, if you only see shades of blue and yellow, then you can't tell apart colours we see as reds, greens and oranges. In old-world primates, and indeed various groups of new-world monkeys as well, the animals 're-evolved' good colour vision, including being able to see yellows and reds against green. A major factor was to find foods – ripe fruit and juicy fresh leaves (which are often red or yellow in the tropics). Crucially, this had another knock-on effect: if these primates could now see more colours for foraging, then they could start to use their excellent vision and bright contrasting colours in mating interactions as well. And they did just that, with modern primate species which have better colour vision tending to be species that use red colours in mating and dominance displays.

While the mandrills have a colour-communication system that can be toned down or turned up as needed, there are other animals that show changes in colour even more dramatically and can switch their display on or off surprisingly quickly. The most well known, perhaps, are the chameleons. These rather odd-looking creatures can be found widely in Africa and the Middle East, but the home of much of their diversity is the island of Madagascar. Here, they exist in extremes. Some, such as *Brookesia micra*, can comfortably fit on top of a fingertip, whereas others, such as Parson's chameleon, can be more than 60 centimetres long. Whatever their size, chameleons have excellent vision.

Their eyes rotate independently and constantly move around, locking on to small insects to eat. The ability to shift their gaze so much enables them to have outstanding 3-D vision and depth perception, perfect for targeting a juicy bug and striking at it with their long sticky tongue. Excellent colour vision enables chameleons to see the world in a rich diversity of hues, but it is their own colour change that is most remarkable – within seconds, an animal can shift from a bright green or blue to a dull brown. We used to think that the main purpose of this skill was for camouflage; we now know otherwise.

Chameleons don't take kindly to rivals coming too close. They rear up, make their body larger, hiss and, of course, change

Chameleons are fabled for their colour changes, like these Jackson's from Kenya. The primary reason, however, is for social signalling, not camouflage.

colour. The way they change colour depends on two things: whether they are dominant or not, and the type of habitat in which they live. Generally, when two rivals meet, after some back and forth movements, the dominant individual becomes brighter, using many colours and patterns to stand out. By contrast, the subordinate signals his capitulation by making his colours duller. The types of colours used are not random.

Dwarf chameleons not only live in different types of forest, but also in more open habitats. The vegetation, therefore, has a range of colours and the light conditions vary considerably, depending on how sunlight is transmitted and scattered. These chameleons, though, are not capable of changing to any and all colours around them. They have a restricted repertoire of hues they can use, and the colours they produce are dictated by the environment in which the species evolved. Species of dwarf chameleon that live in drier forests with more brown vegetation, for example, might adopt a repertoire with more greens and blues, while redder colours can help those in bright green foliage to be more visible. Their base colour helps them to blend in and therefore become less obvious to predators, while the dramatic colour change enables them to stand out, both to rivals and to potential mates.

Colour change in chameleons is controlled by the nervous system, based on what the animal is seeing and responding to, as well as its current state of 'emotion'; that is, whether it is threatened or calm. In the skin of these animals are two types of cell. Chromatophores contain pigments of different colours that absorb different wavelengths of light, and iridophores contain crystals that reflect light. By changing the distribution of these cells, and the pigment within them, the chameleon can adopt a variety of colours and patterns, and quickly.

BEHIND THE SCIENCE

A surprising number of wild animals can change colour or are able to moderate the brightness or darkness of their body. The ways that this is achieved are varied. Primates make certain areas of their skin redder, such as lips, faces or rumps, with the changes usually achieved with alterations in blood flow. As hormones rise or fall, such as during the breeding season, more blood – or blood that is brighter red – is allocated to the body surface and to the patches of skin that are on display. In rhesus macaques, for example, redder and darker faces in females can be a sign that they are receptive.

Animals ranging from insects and crabs through to cuttlefish and chameleons have colour change based on the presence of chromatophores. These contain pigments, such as melanins and carotenoids, and, combined with changing the structure of different tissue layers, they can give rise to whites, blues, reds, greens and yellows. The pigments are held as little packets within the cells, and when the animal needs to change, it either spreads out the pigment or pulls it in tightly. By spreading out lots of melanin, for instance, an animal can become darker in colour. By expanding or contracting different packets of pigment, it can change not only its overall colour, but specific areas or regions of its body. In a few animals, including chameleons, but also cuttlefish, octopus and certain fish, the chromatophore cells are controlled directly by the nervous system. This, in turn, is controlled by the animal's visual system, which responds to what it is currently seeing. In this way, a cuttlefish can morph in seconds to blend in with its background, or modify its appearance to work best at repulsing potential rivals and attracting mates. In most creatures, the changes are controlled by hormones and take hours, days or even weeks, based on what the animal sees, or other influences, such as the arrival of a mating season, when males need to compete. Hormones travel through the body and cause the cells to change.

Even more slowly, some animals change colour with the seasons. Arctic lemmings shift between brown and white as they moult their fur to blend in with summer tundra or winter snow. For mate choice and dominance, when birds like blue tits moult their feathers and grow new ones, the vibrancy of their latest feathers can reflect their condition before they moulted, rather like a window to the past.

The tail of a panther chameleon from Madagascar, with coloration produced by special cells containing pigments.

Overleaf: Not just colour change, but remarkable eyesight enable this male panther chameleon to interact with the environment and other chameleons.

Of course, the need for dominance signalling does not mean that chameleons do not use their powers of change for camouflage too. If an animal has such an ability, then it would seem silly not to use it for defence as well; and indeed, they do. Chameleons can even change their camouflage to work more effectively against whatever predator is threatening them at the time, such as a bird or snake, each having different visual capabilities. Chameleons have another key function of their colour change, and that is to moderate their temperature. When it is hot and the sunlight is intense, they become paler to reflect more heat. Being darker, on the other hand, helps them to absorb more heat when it is colder. Camouflage and thermoregulation, though, are not the primary reasons why chameleons evolved such an ability to change colour: it was for social interactions.

***

Rather than changing appearance, the males of some species have a number of clearly different colour forms, and this can have important implications for their social status and how they behave. Australia is hardly lacking in stunning creatures, and colourful birds abound in the outback, not to mention urban parks. One of Australia's most beautiful is the Gouldian finch. This little bird looks like its body parts have been cobbled together from other species giving rise to a remarkable range of plumage colours, from green and blue to yellow and purple. In such a parched land, access to water is critical, and water sources can be spread far and wide, so there is a strict pecking order that determines which has the first opportunity to quench their thirst. This is revealed by the colour of the bird and, in turn, says something about the type of individual it is.

Gouldian finches do not all look the same. Some have red heads, others black, and a few even have a yellow-orange head. Those with a red head are feisty and aggressive and sit on top of the pile. Black-and yellow-headed birds back off and give the red ones space. Those birds with black heads are less aggressive, but they make up for it in other ways: they explore the environment more and take greater risks. This can put them in elevated danger compared to other birds, but equally it might also mean finding a new food source or nest site. These birds may be forced to take more risks because they are excluded by the red individuals and, perhaps, are able to get away with it as they're a little less visible to predators.

During the breeding season, the birds must pair up and mate but, rather than mixing the colours, the birds much prefer partners of their own colour and therefore individuals that behave in a similar way. Opposites do not attract, so red birds prefer partners with a red head, black with black, and so on. The birds then compete for the best places to nest and, naturally, the red birds get the pick of the best sites.

Being red might sound ideal – the best nest sites and prime access to food and water – so why are all birds not red? The answer is that red has its downside too. For a start, it's hard work. The birds must defend their resources and assert their dominance, and this takes time and energy. It is also stressful. Red birds have higher levels of hormones associated with stress circulating in their body, and this can impair their immune system. As a consequence, red birds have a shorter life expectancy. Black-headed birds, on the other hand, have a slower pace of life – they may be less successful in the short term, but over their entire existence they can more than make up for their inadequacies. Males of this colour type also, freed from the demands of being a dominant individual, spend more time helping to raise the chicks. The result is that two-thirds of the population of this species are birds with black coloration.

Scientists have speculated that the red and black forms may have evolved separately, in populations located in different

geographical regions. At some point, they came back together and now live in mixed populations. It's possible that during their time apart, the different birds evolved the striking contrasts in their behaviour, although there is another idea: the two colour types offer different routes to success, and this depends on how common they are. If a population exists almost entirely of red birds, which are aggressive to one another, it may be better to be black and more subordinate to avoid that aggression, while, at the same time, being adventurous enough to find novel food and nest sites. Eventually, evolution reaches a balance, whereby the relative proportions of each colour type stabilise, and this reflects the advantages and costs of being one colour form or the other.

Quite why birds prefer to mate with the same colour type is still not clear, but there are some clues. Birds of the opposite hue seem to be genetically incompatible, and, if they mate, the offspring have a much lower chance of surviving to adulthood

In Western Australia, a less aggressive black-headed Gouldian finch waits its turn, while a dominant red-headed bird drinks first.

than the progeny of birds of the same type. It's possible that instead of opposites combining to obtain the best of two behaviour types, the birds produce offspring with the worst combination – aggressive risk-takers that simply run into trouble too often for their own good.

Sadly, only 2,500 of these birds remain in the wild, and they are under considerable threat. With the diminishing population, birds of different colour types are having to pair up, resulting in less fit offspring and so damaging the long-term survival of the species. The mother, though, has a trick up her sleeve. She makes the best of a bad job. A red mother paired with a black-headed male, for instance, produces more male chicks in the clutch than if she had been paired with a red partner. Although male birds of these mismatches fare badly, they face less adversity than female chicks. In having more males, therefore, the mother increases the chances that some of her offspring will make it to adulthood. Quite how birds do this is not well understood. In humans, women have two sex chromosomes of the X type, whereas men have one X and one Y. Birds are the opposite, with males having two W chromosomes, and females a W and a Z chromosome. Somehow, and nobody knows how, the mother bird is able to determine whether she releases eggs that have a W or Z chromosome, and thus can manipulate the sex of her offspring. In doing so, she can influence the chances of her chicks' survival.

* * *

Males of multiple colour types also occur in some fish. In the waters in and around Lake Tanganyika in Tanzania and Zambia lives a remarkable species. Like many cichlids, it is very colourful with a rich social life; but Burton's mouthbrooder is unusual in that the males come in several different, and reversible, colour types. The reason for this is down to dominance and territorial behaviour.

In this species, some of the males are dominant and hold a territory, while others are subordinate and do not. The subordinates are a dull green-brown camouflage colour, looking rather like females. The dominant males are highly aggressive towards other fish and are vivid yellow or blue. They comprise around one-third of a population, and they display on a lek-type system, each male holding a small patch on the lake bed, where rivals are chased away and females enticed. The subordinate males, meanwhile, gain from being inconspicuous. They form mixed shoals with the females and do not try to reproduce, but in doing so, they have greater access to food. When chased away by a dominant male, these meek individuals always flee. Aggressive males, on the other hand, will gesture back and forth to one another in ritualistic, hostile displays, and these encounters can sometimes turn into physical violence, including biting and chasing. When ready to breed, females prefer these dominant, colourful males.

The colour of the males, and the behaviour they show, can quickly change. When a previously dominant male loses to a rival, usually a bigger fish, he quickly dulls in colour and loses his aggressive manner. Previously dull males that win, however, quickly – within a few minutes – become aggressive and develop a black band across the eye. Gradually, they also become colourful. The change is underpinned, in large part, by an area of the brain that controls sexual behaviour. As subordinates, the fish are constantly being pushed around and have high levels of stress hormones. These suppress activity in those key brain regions. When the fish escape domination and become dominant themselves, the levels of stress hormones drop, and sexual brain activity increases. Following this, the reproductive organs can develop. They become enlarged and more active, and so enable the fish to breed. It means, the behaviour of these fish is very much in tune with their social environment. The top dog not only shows off his status with bright colours, but he acts accordingly. When the dominant male is removed, others take on the role.

The coloration of male Burton's mouthbrooders can change depending on whether they are winning or losing.

Quite why some males are dull and cryptic, while others are vivid, seems clear enough, but why do dominant males come in two colours? In many populations, the proportion of yellow individuals and blue types seems about the same and, strangely, males not only switch from camouflaged to vibrant colours, but also they can convert from blue to yellow and vice versa. Females appear to show little preference for either, so the reason probably lies elsewhere. It comes back to aggression. In general, males act more aggressively to fish of the opposite colour, so, for example, a yellow male is more hostile to a blue rival than he is to a fellow yellow fish. Yellow fish also tend to be dominant over blue ones, driven by higher levels of hormones that control aggressive behaviour and potentially give them an advantage in the short term. By contrast, blue fish are more aggressive to those cryptic subordinate individuals swimming with shoals of females; subordinate males that might one day try to usurp them. Although less dominant, blue males gain weight faster than yellow fish, and this might allow them to maintain dominant positions for longer and see off potential new rivals.

A male Burton's mouthbrooder from Tanzania entices a female using his body coloration.

So, while it is not entirely clear why the dominant males come in two types, and why they switch between them, it may come down to differences in the way that they behave and the different benefits of where they focus their time and aggression.

*** *** ***

Cichlids are studied by biologists, not only for their colour, but also because hundreds of species have evolved in a very short time. Similarly, another large and impressive group of rapidly evolving vertebrates is the *Anolis* lizards, predominantly found in Central and South America. This group shows how animals can spread quickly into new geographical areas, resulting in a variety of species occupying different habitats. There are around 400 species, with 150 in the Caribbean alone. Many islands have their own species and, on a few, several species might live together in the same place, although some have become specialised for life nearer the forest floor, while others are adapted to a life in the trees.

When communicating, Golfo Dulce anoles from Costa Rica combine excellent camouflage with the ability to display brightly coloured dewlaps.

BEHIND THE SCIENCE

In the natural world, some groups of animals have diversified greatly, with many species occupying a broad range of habitats. In evolutionary terms, such 'adaptive radiations' can sometimes occur very quickly. One of the most famous examples is Darwin's Galápagos finches, where many species have evolved on the different islands and have a variety of beak shapes to exploit the varied foods present on each island. *Anolis* lizards are another group, with similar, but distinct, species living on neighbouring islands. Frequently, adaptation to different habitats is reflected in features that make a species well suited to its local environment, and colour can be a major part of such divergence. *Anolis* that live in lower parts of the forest, for example, tend to be brown in order to blend in with the dry litter and tree trunks. By contrast, those species occupying parts of the forest higher up tend to be green, to match the foliage. Over time, different behaviours arise too, and individuals from different groups may stop breeding with one another, and therefore begin to form separate species. Gradually, the group radiates into numerous species across an entire region, like *Anolis* in the Caribbean.

Sometimes, the colour of animals and the quality of their vision may play an important role in driving adaptive radiations. Cichlid fish are diverse and colourful and abundant in the African Great Lakes; in fact, 1,500 or so species exist there. They have diversified as a group in a very short space of time, with many species arising in just a few hundred thousand years. Some species live closer to the surface, while others are found deeper down, and these different regions of the lakes have contrasting light conditions. In Tanzania's Lake Victoria, the light becomes more brown-orange in colour with greater depth. Those species living lower down have visual systems that are better at seeing colours in this part of the spectrum – they are more sensitive to orange and red light. To take advantage of this, and to be more easily seen, the males become a vivid red, an aid to communication. Closer to the top of the lake the water is less red, and other colours, such as blues, can be seen more easily, so species living in these surface waters are more sensitive to shortwave blue light and, to aid communication, bodies tend to be a metallic blue-grey.

The light conditions in the lake have driven the evolution of the visual systems of each species, so they are more sensitive to certain colours. This, in turn, has influenced the evolution of their body colours, with males displaying colour signals that are most readily seen. As we would expect, the fish are more responsive to the colours they detect most effectively, including those used during mating by their own species, so that different groups tend not to mate with one another. The upshot is that light conditions, coloration and behaviour all seem to have played an important role in the formation of many cichlid species. Competition among males might have also played a substantial role, because if males of one species show more aggression towards particular colour types – by directing most aggression to red males during feeding interactions for instance – then it may benefit males of other groups to be another colour, such as blue, to avoid hostilities. The outcome is that the cichlids diverge in coloration within the same areas, potentially even splitting into many species.

Anolis lizards also vary greatly in the colours they use for communication. While their main body is often green or brown, for camouflage, *Anolis* possess a striking feature called the dewlap. This extending flap of skin from under the chin is adorned with bright colours and patterns and plays a significant role in 'talking' to others of their own kind. The dewlaps vary among species, sometimes playing a role in how individuals recognise their species from others, but they also play a major role in territorial defence. *Anolis* lizards are well known for their vibrant displays, often combining extensions of their dewlap with amusing body movements.

Territorial defence in *Anolis* is very important. The green anole, for example, can be very feisty towards those that are not welcome. Male green anoles keep guard of up to three females present in their mini realms, and the owners will fight especially hard when the territory is more valuable. The males have a bright red dewlap, but those on females are more modest: smaller and pinker in colour, and might play a role in social interactions, such as in competition for food. Should one male venture into the territory of another, the resident will extend his dewlap and bob up and down. If the warning fails, he will chase the intruder away, and they may even come to blows, biting one another until one submits.

Dewlap colours vary greatly, not just the hue, but also pattern and overall size, but why some dewlaps are green and black while others are purple, blue, green or even white is not well understood. It might be that this diversity of colours is used to attract mates, or that different forms enable the lizards to recognise their own species. Alternatively, it may simply be that all the colours we observe are effective in achieving the same communication function, given that *Anolis* have excellent colour vision and that, simply by chance, different species have adopted one colour

By extending his red dewlap only when needed, a brown anole can defend his territory, but not compromise his camouflage at other times.

instead of another. That said, one of the curious features of *Anolis* dewlaps is that the colour tends to depend on where in the habitat the species spends most of its time.

Species living deeper in shaded forest tend to have yellow dewlaps, whereas those living in brighter conditions are more likely to have red or orange ones. It seems that yellow colours stand out more against the green leaves and forest lighting under low light conditions, whereas red or orange are better in brighter light. Indeed, lizards are more likely to turn and respond towards red colours in bright light and yellow colours in dim conditions, than the other way round. Scientists studying the lizards have also noticed that the dewlaps appear to glow in the forest gloom. This is no accident, and the flaps of many species are translucent, so they let through some of the sunlight coming from behind the animal. The effect is to make the colour signal brighter and more distinct from the background. It is a trick that is especially valuable in darker environments.

The habitat can also have a big influence on the way *Anolis* use their dewlap in behavioural displays. The male yellow-chinned anole from Puerto Rico – which, as the name suggests, has a glowing yellow dewlap – advertises territory ownership by displaying on the lower trunks of trees in the forest. Alongside its colourful dewlap, it performs a ritualised head-bobbing sequence to ward off others, but first, the lizard will often do something else: it'll perform push-ups on the tree, raising and lowering its body in a jerky fashion. Lizards don't always do this; in fact, they are much more likely to start with push-ups when the environment is darker, or if it is a windy day. The push-up sequence is there to attract attention before the other moving displays are performed. When it's dark the main display is less likely to be seen by rivals. Likewise, if the vegetation in the background is constantly being blown around by a strong breeze, seeing a signal based on movement is harder; so the push-ups alert others who may be watching to pay attention, before the main territory defence signals are given. It's rather like shouting 'hi' across the road to a friend to get their attention before saying what we want them to know. It works, too. In gloomy or gusty conditions, rivals are much more likely to see and respond to the main display if it is preceded by push-ups. So the colourful and charismatic nature of these lizards has arisen, at least in part, to communicate with one another in the varied forest environments and conditions in which they live.

* * *

As we have learnt, not all animals communicate in colours and patterns of light that are visible to us. Invertebrates, in particular, tend to do things rather differently. Of these, many types of crabs are thought to have relatively poor colour vision. They see fewer colours than us, and their compound eyes show them a world that to us would seem blurry, rather than sharp and defined. A few crabs have better colour vision, including some species of fiddler crab, which are themselves often decked out in bright colours, their costumes used to communicate with one another. In some species, the vividness of their colours is greater when there are fewer predators about. Individuals can raise or lower their brightness based on the conflicting needs of hiding from those predators, particularly birds, and signalling to other crabs.

Fiddler crabs live in burrows on mudflats and among mangroves. The many and varied species can be found right across the globe, from the coasts of Brazil to the mangroves of Southeast Asia and the beaches of Australia. Their world is largely horizontal and so, to see as much as possible, their eyes are elevated on stalks, raising them up above the ground. It also

allows the crab to divide the world into above and on the horizon. Things that appear above the horizon are likely to be predators, whereas those that occur along it are other crabs. The fiddler's eyes are also well tuned to enable the crab to effectively resolve objects in a vertical plane, such as something heading straight for it. So the raising of the eyes on stalks, their elongated shape and the arrangement of the light-sensitive cells allow the crab to see things with a wide field of view and to detect threats that might be heading towards it.

Fiddler crabs are in many regards rather comical creatures. The males sport a greatly enlarged claw, which in some species is so big that it can weigh half of the male's entire bodyweight. As the crabs emerge from their burrows, they begin waving their oversized claws to communicate. Their bright colours might look very easy to spot, but it is not as easy as you might think to pick out individuals in the crowded mudflats, with everyone waving. It's a situation made especially challenging given that crabs often coexist in high densities, with a mixture of species, and they're all waving and moving around at the same time. To make things worse, the bright colours can blend into the sandy background. Even so, fiddler crabs can spot another crab from 2 metres away and a small bird in the sky from 10 to 15 metres, but they don't see detail very well like we do. They do, however, have another trick for detecting threats and rivals, aside from the arrangement of their eyes.

Regardless of their level of colour perception, many crabs have a skill that we lack: they can see and respond to changes in polarised light. This can help greatly in coastal habitats, where light is reflected back from the moist surface and patches of water on mudflats, not least in the tropics where the sun is strong. One of the benefits of polarisation vision is that it can be excellent at enhancing contrast and reducing glare. Think of how much clearer the ocean looks, and how much more you can see beneath

Elevated eyes, big claws and bright colours help fiddler crabs to communicate across mudflats and mangroves.

the waves, when wearing polarising sunglasses. Many features in the environment also stand out. A white predatory bird circling in the sky, for example, can blend in with the light background behind it, but it presents a clear silhouette when seen in polarised light. This is because the bird's body does not reflect polarised light, and so it looks dark. When a predator comes too close, the crabs can use this to spot it and then dart for cover. They can also better see rivals. While the crabs themselves generally fall below the horizon in the crab's field of view, the waving claws can be higher and so are easier to pick out.

The crabs need to communicate as they have prime real estate to defend. Each male crab digs out a burrow and protects his small patch from rivals. The burrow offers a safe refuge from threats, somewhere to dart into when at risk, and the crab collects balls of mud, each filled with algae, bacteria and detritus that they store and feed on later. The burrow is also an important place to attract

a female, and some fiddler crabs even build mud structures next door to attract her attention, so he must keep it safe from rivals.

A crab spots the pattern of a rival coming towards him by using polarisation. It's an early warning system, so the burrow owner is ready and prepared to defend his site. The huge claw may be a heavy burden, but it's a formidable weapon. During the fight, the large claws are used to push and try to flip over one another, until one crab backs down and leaves. A female understandably prefers males with bigger, brighter claws. She is attracted initially to the size and motion of the swaying claw – again, something much easier to see when using polarised light, so it contrasts with the background. When she gets closer, she can more readily assess the male's body-colour intensity and whether he fits the part. At this time in the ritual, the crabs play another trick with colour. They don't have their vivid markings placed just anywhere, but instead their bodies are adorned most vibrantly in areas where another crab is most likely to see them – their 'faces' and claws. Their backs tend to be duller – all the better to avoid attracting predators.

Of all the animals on Earth, perhaps the most bizarre looking are the mantis shrimps, exotic marine creatures that have torn up the vision and communication rule book, taking colour and polarisation to a whole new level. They possess two huge specialised eyes that move and rotate independently and, seemingly, in almost any direction. They come in a kaleidoscope of colours and patterns, and they carry some of the fiercest weapons in nature. There are 400 or so species around the world, and they are all notoriously aggressive. In an attack, they use specialised front appendages – some have spears for stabbing and impaling, while others have club-shaped appendages for

A male fiddler crab uses his enlarged claw to display. Some crabs can see colour and also detect polarised light. A special polarisation camera shows how the high contrast between the polarised beach and the crab's unpolarised carapace may help it spot predators and other crabs from afar.

smashing things. By wielding their weapons 50 times faster than the blink of an eye and with a force strong enough to break glass, they create a shock wave that can stun their unfortunate victims.

There's no doubt that mantis shrimps are among the most colourful creatures on Earth. The ultra-flamboyant and aptly named peacock mantis shrimp can be found across the entire Indo-Pacific region. It dwells in burrows in shallow waters down to 30 or 40 metres depth, among the rubble at the bases of coral reefs. The species is a wonderful mixture of green, red, blue, white, orange and purple, but it is their vision and eyes that are of interest to scientists. While humans have three types of cones in the retina for colour vision, some mantis shrimps have between twelve and sixteen different light receptors, including several tuned specifically to various frequencies of ultraviolet light. Paradoxically, this doesn't actually mean that mantis shrimps see more colours than we do – in fact, it's the opposite.

Mantis shrimps may be feisty and not the best choice of animals to keep together, but they have valuable traits for understanding vision. For one thing, they can be trained to perform tasks. In the laboratory, mantis shrimps have been taught to make choices between two options, allowing us to investigate how and when they can tell two colours apart. In the tests, it came as a surprise to discover that, even though they have all those different light receptors, they are actually worse at discriminating colours than humans. Their receptor cells have a direct line to the brain and, unlike nearly all other known animals, they don't seem to compare their outputs, but simply react based on whichever cell types are stimulated. The question is why these curious creatures do things so differently. In truth, it really is a mystery, but for mantis shrimps speed is key, and having a visual system like theirs enables them to encode a

Few animals rival the colours and bizarre eyes of the mantis
shrimp, like this peacock mantis shrimp in the Philippines.

modest range of colours, but lightning fast. This enables them to react to prey, mates and threats in an instant.

The vision of mantis shrimps is also well suited to where they live. Species in deeper water, which in clear ocean habitats tends to be bluer, have a visual system that is more sensitive to blue light. Those closer to the surface have vision that sees a wider range of colours. Even within the same species, individuals living deeper down shift their colour perception so they can see blue better. Mantis shrimp larvae start life able to detect a wide spectrum of light, but those individuals that settle deeper down in the ocean have the cells in their eyes change to be more sensitive to bluer light. The way in which their vision is tuned helps the mantis shrimps to most effectively see the colours that are visible in the places where they live.

Mantis shrimps have another astonishing skill. They see and use polarised light; and not just any form, but circular polarised light. As a wave of light travels, it oscillates in a certain direction, such as up and down or side to side, giving it a certain angle of polarisation. Many animals can distinguish between these angles

and the amount of light that is present in particular orientations. Many species, from dragonflies to fish (though not humans), can tell apart features of polarised light, such as the main angles present and how much the light is dominated by certain angles of polarisation. In some cases, however, light waves travel more like a corkscrew, where the angle of polarisation rotates in a clockwise or anticlockwise direction. Mantis shrimps can detect this and discriminate it from other types of polarised light, and, as far as we know, they are the only animal that can do this. One of the benefits is that using colour patterns that also have polarised light properties can increase the visibility of visual signals under water. To be able to see different types of polarised light, an animal must have cells in the eye that can distinguish the different angles of polarisation, so the animal is able to compare them. Mantis shrimps have such receptors, but they also have another skill to see polarised light effectively.

Anyone who has watched a mantis shrimp can't help but notice the extreme flexibility with which it moves its eyes. One eye can be moved around and rotated to look in different directions and

A polarisation camera reveals how the large antennal scales of the male peacock mantis shrimp reflect polarised light, and he may use these in displays to females or to defend burrows.

angles, independently of the other eye. One of the benefits of this is being able to align different cells to best detect any polarisation and enhance the visual signal. It's rather like having a dynamic system that can change with time to optimally detect what polarised light is present in the environment. When a mantis shrimp is rotating its eyes, it's getting a better look at any patterns of polarisation that might be around.

A major benefit of polarisation for mantis shrimps, especially being able to see circular polarised light, is in communication with potential mates and rivals. On parts of their body, such as tails, antennae and the paddle-shaped antennal scales, individuals exhibit special patterns that can be seen only with a visual system sensitive to circular polarisation. These patterns can differ between males and females, but they are also used to deter threatening neighbours. Invisible to all other animals, circular polarised light patterns act as a sign to rivals that potential burrows are occupied. Individuals rarely leave the safety of their burrow, but at times they must do so to find mates or search further away for food. This brings them into conflict with one another, especially rival males. By displaying polarisation signals, however, mantis shrimps can avoid some of this conflict.

Some species have another curious feature that adds yet more to the diverse ways in which they communicate: their bodies fluoresce. When this occurs, light of relatively short wavelengths (like ultraviolet or blue) is absorbed and reemitted at longer wavelengths, such as yellow. Fluorescence is actually quite common in nature, not least in a variety of animals on tropical reefs, from corals to fish. In many cases, fluorescence may have no function at all, being merely a by-product of other processes happening in the body. It is also too subtle to be seen under most bright daylight conditions, when full sunlight swamps its effect. However, in environments that are relatively dim and rich in ultraviolet and blue light, fluorescence may amplify the vividness of some colour signals. These types of environments are exactly where mantis shrimps live, and the fluorescent effect of their markings is heightened at greater depths. When a mantis shrimp is vulnerable and antagonised by a rival male or a potential predator it will perform a threat display, rearing up and displaying its appendages. In the process, it shows off its fluorescent coloration.

For these unworldly and heavily armed animals, getting into a fight would be potentially lethal. Instead, they fend off rivals with secret flashes of polarisation and colours enhanced by fluorescence, all detected by a super-fast visual system.

*** * ***

Gaining access to food, potential mates and territories with important resources is of great value to many animals. Securing access is just half the job, because a successful individual must keep away other suitors for as long as he can. Fights in nature are costly, and not only to the loser. The victor may have vanquished his latest rival but, if he sustains a terrible injury or is weakened too much, fending off the next threat might not be possible, or injuries may even be fatal. While many animals, especially males, are equipped with weapons and aggression, it is therefore much better to win the day through a simple show of force. Colour performs this role extremely well, not least because it can be a valuable indicator of the strength and vitality of the bearer. In many creatures, it can also be adjusted, based on current status or rank, or even condition. In reality, only when two creatures are well matched does physical violence tend to escalate most. There are, however, other important reasons why many animals in nature are showy, and one of those is to deter not rivals, but predators.

CHAPTER FOUR

WARNING SIGNALS

Dangling in a small web, with a jet-black body and iconic red hourglass on its underside, a black widow spider is as unmistakable as it is infamous; yet, despite its strong venom and devilish reputation, the spider rarely inflicts harm on humans, and when it does, the bite is in defence of its own life. The red and black markings present a strong visual contrast to the eyes of predators, such as birds and other small vertebrates, which might mistake the small spider for an easy meal.

It's a warning: 'Don't try to attack, or it may do you more harm than me.' The coloration of the spider is well directed, since it often hangs upside down with the red marking pointing upwards towards a threat coming from above. At the same time, the red patch is small enough that most insects, which often lack good vision for these colours, don't see the marking easily and still blunder into the spider's web as prey themselves.

Charles Darwin sometimes got himself into a bit of a fluster when his observations did not initially appear to fit his theories. One such case was when he was working on his theory of sexual selection. Here, he was examining how bright colours in nature were used for show, proposing that they were generally used by males to attract females, but he hit a snag: many animals in

Red is the colour of danger on the underside of this black widow spider.

nature are brightly coloured at times when they are not ready to breed. The caterpillars of butterflies and moths, for example, don't reproduce until they have metamorphosed into the adult form, so, why do the caterpillars of many species need bright colours? For an answer, Darwin turned to fellow naturalist and explorer Alfred Russel Wallace, who had independently arrived at an outline of evolution very similar to Darwin's theory of natural selection. Wallace knew the answer – many animals are brightly coloured to warn would-be predators that they are 'disgusting morsels'. Their bright colours are a sign that they are toxic or have dangerous spines, venom or some other such defence, and any attack might do significant harm to the predator. The aggressor should look elsewhere. Darwin found this solution ingenious and, ever since, scientists have been studying how warning colours work.

In the modern world, we often tend to associate colours such as red and yellow with signs of danger and even widely use them to grab attention, from road signs to the markings on emergency vehicles, but this use of conspicuous colours to highlight warnings was adopted in nature long before humans arose. Our sense of heightened awareness with reds and yellows comes partly from our vision being well suited to detect these hues, but also probably owing to an inbuilt cautiousness towards such signals, stemming from deep in our evolutionary past. Creatures all around the world use vivid contrasting patterns to tell others to take note. There is more to warning colours than just standing out, however, as the specific form that they take in nature varies and reflects a diversity of selection pressures, from denoting exactly how toxic an animal is, to serving a dual function, from mate choice to even, surprisingly, camouflage.

***

While frogs in many temperate regions tend to favour green and brown patterns for camouflage, in the tropics they can be extraordinarily colourful. Chief among these are the poison dart frogs. As their name implies, local tribes in South America have regularly used these frogs to anoint the tips of their hunting spears with potent poison, which the frogs produce through their skin.

Poison frogs tend to be small, frequently just a few centimetres in length, and they could make a tasty morsel for a range of predators, from snakes and lizards to birds and even spiders; but, as Wallace realised, the colour of these frogs sends a powerful warning to predators that might be foolish enough to attack them. Antagonists like birds, with their excellent colour perception, see the variety of reds, oranges, yellows and blacks as signs of danger. Should they have an encounter with a frog and live to tell the tale, they remember the colour and pattern and so which ones to avoid in the future. The frogs obtain their defences from their diet – eating mites, ants, beetles and millipedes, and using chemicals found in their prey to synthesise a poison that the frogs make in glands in the skin. When at risk, they quickly secrete the toxins.

Many poison frogs are well known to be variable in colour; not just among different species, but even individuals of the same species. This sometimes conveys just how dangerous they are. In the rainforests of Central and South America, lives the strawberry dart frog – less than 2 centimetres in size, but often super colourful. Up to about 30 different colour forms of this species occur, ranging from yellow–green and black, to bright fiery red. They have been closely studied in the Bocas del Toro archipelago, off the northwest coast of Panama, where the frogs on each island have distinctive colours. Over thousands of years, changes in sea level caused the islands to become split off from

Poison dart frogs have bright colours that warn would-be predators they are toxic. These three frogs are the same species of strawberry poison dart frog, but their isolation on different islands in Panama has meant each has evolved a different colour.

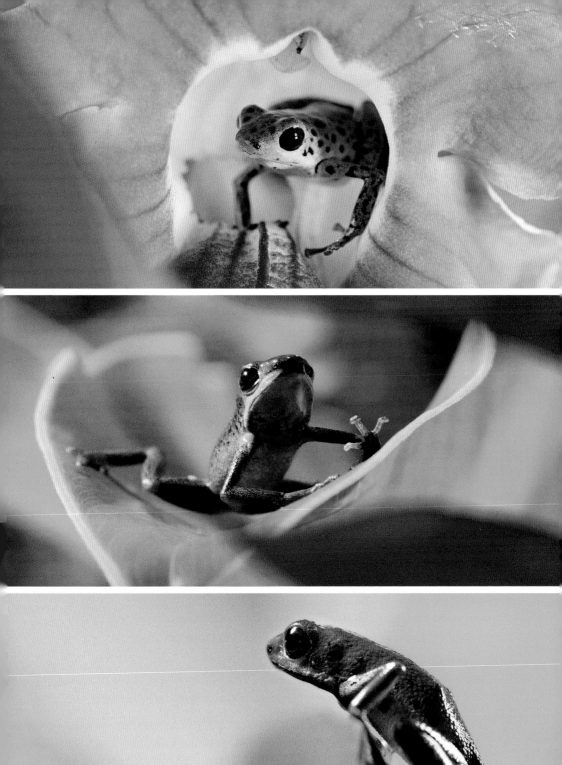

the mainland. Prior to this, the frogs were probably all much the same colour, but, over time, those on different islands evolved new appearances, with some frogs becoming more poisonous. The more dangerous ones began to signal this by increasing the vibrancy of their coloration, such that islands possessing the most toxic frogs have the most vivid specimens. Individuals on the island of Solarte are bright orange and about 40 times more toxic than a much duller yellow-green frog on the neighbouring island of Colón. Defence against predators is not the only reason for their diversity in colour. Frogs on separate islands have also developed preferences for potential mates of different colour types, and this has further contributed to the island populations looking increasingly different from one another. More conspicuous individuals can sometimes be more dominant and so favoured by females.

Female poison dart frogs are attentive mothers. They lay eggs in tiny pools of water that collect in bromeliad plants. Here, with one to a pond, the egg and then tadpole develop, but in

Poison dart frogs have a variety of potential predators. Here, a strawberry frog from Panama takes cover from a crab.

such a small pool the food options are scarce. A few mosquito larvae and other tiny creatures are not sufficient to sustain the ravenous tadpole. Remarkably, the mother returns regularly to each of her developing young, and into each pond she lays an unfertilised egg for them to eat. The tadpole is able to recognise the smell, look and vibrations made by its mother, versus those of a potential predator. When the cues match those of a visiting frog, rather than a spider or lizard, for example, the tadpole comes to the surface to beg. Receiving an egg carries a dual benefit, partly in nutrition, but also because the eggs are laced with toxins that the growing tadpoles add into their own bodies. By the time the baby frog enters the outside world, it is already well protected and its colour patterns are already on display.

When you see their gaudy costumes in a guidebook, it's hard to believe that poison dart frogs are not always as visible as we might expect. Many are covered with elaborate patterns, with black stripes and blotches, so, when seen from a distance in the forest, the bright colours and dark markings blend together to

Pools of rainwater that gather in bromeliads make ideal homes for strawberry poison dart frogs to lay their eggs. Mothers remember each pool and revisit them later.

match the environment quite well, and some of the markings help the animal to further blend into the shadows; yet, close up, the frogs stand out strikingly well – they are using defences that are dependent upon how far away the predator is standing or flying. There is always a risk, of course, that being colourful will simply invite an attack, perhaps from an especially bold, misguided or naïve foe, risking the life of the frog. Better to go unnoticed if they can and then fall back on their bright colours and defences should a predator get too close.

* * *

Obtaining defences from the diet is a common route to toxicity right across nature, and there are some unusual examples. Native people across the world have long noted that a variety of birds are best avoided, as they don't taste good. Over the years, naturalists have pondered whether some birds are unpleasant to eat, not due to simply tasting bad, but because they contain noxious chemicals. Stories abound of early scientists and explorers taste-testing birds to determine whether this was true. The famous British zoologist and explorer Hugh B. Cott noted that some birds seemed to be avoided by predators, and in the 1940s he presented a variety of birds to hornets, cats and people to test their palatability. Cott suggested that some species were less pleasant to eat than others, and that this may be signalled by the birds' colour. Nonetheless, while many vertebrates had potent chemical defences – the venom of snakes and other reptiles, fish and even the odd mammal, such as the platypus, and the poisons of frogs – birds seemed not to be among them.

In 1989, everything changed. Exploring the avian fauna of New Guinea, ornithologists captured some pitohui birds in their nets. These creatures are striking in appearance, often with red-brown and black feathers arranged in blocks over the body parts. In the course of handling the animals, the scientists touched their mouths and noted a following sense of numbness, burning and the desire to sneeze. As it happens, the locals knew only too well that the birds were not good to eat, labelling them 'rubbish birds', which should only be eaten if skinned and prepared in a certain way.

By 1992, three species of pitohui had been shown to contain a potent chemical called batrachotoxin, the same neurotoxin found in poison dart frogs from South America. Soon after, more species were added, and in all cases the most toxic parts of the birds were the skin and feathers. Of the six species of pitohui that have been tested, all are toxic, to a lesser or greater extent. The source of the toxins is very likely the birds' diet. Although pitohui are omnivores, consuming fruit much of the time, they also eat invertebrates, and one group of flower beetles are known to be very toxic with the same poisons. The beetles have been found in the stomach contents of the birds. In fact, they may, at least in part, be the same source of some of the infamous defences of poison frogs (the frogs also obtain their toxins from ants and mites). Pitohui species also often emit a smell that is strong and 'sour' – another key sign to warn predators, alongside their colour.

Found in lowland forests, the hooded pitohui is the most highly defended of all the species – small amounts of its skin may contain enough poison to kill lesser animals, although the potency of all pitohui species is much less than that of the poison frogs. The hooded pitohui is a splendid bird to observe, its head, tail and wings being black, with the rest of the bird's body a strong brown-red. Across the pitohui species, the potency of each bird's chemical defence varies with the geographic region and the exact population, probably depending on their regional diet. These birds often breed cooperatively in groups and even form mixed species flocks. Grouping together may help them to enhance the salience of their coloration.

Quite why the pitohui is one of the few birds to contain toxins is not yet clear, but the patterns they show parallel many other groups, not least species of butterflies, frogs and ladybirds. Sometimes, the pitohui species share a similar appearance, the resemblance to one another helping each to warn predators more effectively. As with other animals wearing warning colours, the reduction in the variety of colour patterns means that predators have fewer signals that they must study, so they learn faster and, as a result, a smaller number of birds needs to be attacked in order to teach the predators about their defence. Similarly, less toxic species of pitohui seem to be a duller colour than the more poisonous birds. While the hooded pitohui is particularly toxic and relatively consistent in appearance across its range, another potent species, the variable pitohui, can be anything from green to brown-red to black and orange, depending where it lives on the huge island. However, where the two species overlap the most, they look very similar. This suggests that they mutually benefit from educating the same set of predators with the same warning signals.

The prevailing assumption is that pitohui chemical defences evolved to save them from predators. In the depths of the New Guinea rainforests this, however, is not easy to prove, especially if the predators have learnt to avoid the birds, and attacks are rare. They are most likely under threat from snakes and birds of prey and, while the adults are clearly defended, it has also been suggested that the toxins may rub off from their feathers and onto their eggs, helping to protect their unhatched young from mammalian nest predators. Further evidence that the birds' plumage and toxins act as warning signals comes from the observation that a number of other unrelated and harmless birds

Few birds are known to be toxic to predators, but the red warbler from Mexico (top) and hooded pitohui (bottom) from Papua New Guinea are striking exceptions.

seem to match the appearance of the most toxic pitohui, in order to be protected themselves. The potent chemicals, however, might also play a role in getting rid of parasitic lice and ticks – pitohui have some of the lowest levels of infestation found across similar birds in their habitat, suggesting the toxins afford some protection here too.

Not long after the finding that pitohui are chemically defended, another bird of New Guinea, the blue-capped ifrit, was also discovered to deposit related toxins into its skin and feathers. This bird, coming from an ancient lineage not closely related to the pitohui, is also endemic to the island and eats only insects, again perhaps consuming the potent flower beetles. Striking differences exist between these two groups. The ifrit is found in high mountain forests, barely overlapping with the pitohui. Appearances are not similar either, with the ifrit being mostly a dull brown and black, with a head covered with a blue ring around the crown and a black cap. The ifrit certainly does not display the classic warning signals that other terrestrial creatures favour, but maybe the blue is a clear sign high up where it lives, with light conditions rich in blue and ultraviolet light. Beyond this, a group of shrikethrushes has also been shown to be toxic and is also found in … New Guinea. Toxic birds from beyond this biodiversity hotspot also exist, including the red warbler from Mexico, which was classed as inedible by the Aztecs, and the spur-winged goose from sub-Saharan Africa, which is poisonous due to it eating blister beetles. Dozens more birds have been shown, in one way or another, potentially to be unpalatable, but not necessarily toxic or harmful. Only more time will tell whether these birds are evolutionary anomalies, or whether many other birds pack a powerful punch.

* * *

Ladybird beetles are wonderfully diverse in form and potency, and they also have vivid colours to show they are toxic. We might sometimes assume that all ladybirds are red with black spots, such as the familiar seven-spot, but this is by no means true. Across the world, over 3,500 species of ladybird have been described, living in the forests of South America to the savannahs of Africa. In the UK alone there are 46 resident species, of which just over half are brightly marked and colourful. Many diverge from the classic seven-spot ladybird look. The orange ladybird, for instance, is covered in white spots set against a bright orange body, whereas the pine ladybird is jet black with four small red spots. Many species also come in several types, or morphs, including the two-spot ladybird, which can either be red with black spots, or black with red spots. Ladybirds not only have toxins inside their body, should they end up inside an enemy's mouth, but they also exude a substance with an unpleasant taste and smell by 'reflex bleeding', as anyone who has too roughly handled a ladybird can attest to. In an ideal world, predators will be put off even before they are tempted to take a bite.

Within some species of ladybird, such as the seven-spot, those individuals with brighter or redder coloration are more toxic. Like poison frogs, the toxins that ladybirds synthesise stem from their diet. So too, does their colour. Carotenoids, the pigments that produce reds and oranges, are a key ingredient in maintaining a healthy body and are gathered from food, alongside the key chemical alkaloids that are components of their toxins; so a ladybird that has fed well on aphids and been able to produce lots of toxins will be a brighter red. Among species, it is a similar story, although the types of toxins the ladybirds use can vary. Some species, such as the larch ladybird, are relatively dull and not especially poisonous, whereas others, like two-spot and orange ladybirds, are both colourful and

highly toxic. Hunters – birds in particular – know this and avoid eating beetles that are more vivid and dangerous. They are much more wary of attacking two-spot than larch ladybirds.

Remarkably, even the eggs of ladybirds portray their defence. Mothers inject chemical defences as they produce them and, at the same time, insert carotenoid pigments to make the clutch stand out in glorious orange. Against green leaves, it's a clear warning to anything that may fancy a light lunch. Unfortunately, for some ladybirds, things are not so simple because some predators, including individuals of their own kind, still eat the eggs. The larvae of two-spot ladybirds are known to cannibalise

Harlequin ladybirds are invasive in Europe and well protected from predators, their diverse patterns warning enemies of their toxins. They also consume the eggs of native ladybirds.

eggs of their own species, and in doing so can acquire some of the toxins for themselves. By contrast, the toxins in the eggs can deter other predatory ladybird species, including the harlequin ladybird, as the poisons retard the growth of the harlequin larvae. So, a mother two-spot ladybird must find the right balance between lacing the eggs with toxins to put off predatory harlequins and other species, but not attract cannibalistic larvae of her own species.

* * *

Making eggs unpalatable is a strategy used by several animals, including an aquatic creature from the wetlands of Argentina. Among the vegetation sticking up from the water can be found clumps of hundreds of bright pink balls. Standing out vividly against the green backdrop, these are the eggs of apple snails. The bright coloration comes from carotenoid pigments, and it conveys to potential predators that consuming these objects would not be wise. Normally, the eggs of many animals are an easy and nutrient-rich meal but, as with the ladybirds, a few species have developed strategies to protect them. Apple snails lace them with a potent poison that can cause serious neurobiological harm to anything that consumes them, including to the central nervous system of mammals. Furthermore, the eggs also contain a powerful enzyme inhibitor that stops the eggs from being digested, even if some creature is foolish enough to eat them. So it's a double whammy: the predator struggles to gain much by nutrition from the eggs, and it gets a powerful dose of toxin instead. Only one animal is said to ever consume apple snail eggs, the notoriously aggressive, highly invasive and very adaptable fire ant.

Species of apple snail have now unfortunately been unleashed into non-native countries, from North America to Southeast Asia, in part from the aquarium trade, when people have released them from tanks into the wild. The snails compete with native species and damage water plants and even rice fields. Owing to their serious defences, few native animals can halt the spread of apple snails, and they are now considered as one of the most serious invasive species on the planet.

✳ ✳ ✳

Few animals can devour the bright pink eggs of apple snails, which can be found in clusters close to water in their native range in South America.

Not all animals gain their defences solely from their diet. Around coastal areas of the UK, in the summer sunshine, flashes of colour can be seen as moths flutter over thistle and knapweed flowers. Six-spot burnet moths, like many other burnet moth species, are adorned with shiny metallic blue-black wings dotted with bright red spots that sparkle in the sunlight. They are some of the most beautiful moths found in Britain and brazenly go about their business in full daylight. They can do this because few animals ever try to eat them. While birds in particular might consider the moths a tasty meal, most are wise enough to avoid them, for the burnet moths have powerful toxins known to contain that most infamous of poisons, cyanide.

As larvae, the insects often acquire the cyanide-containing toxins from their diet, with the yellow and black caterpillars feeding on bird's-foot trefoil. Rare among insects, however, the burnet moth larvae can also make their own toxins, even when not feasting on the appropriately laden host plants. Having both routes means that the larvae, and the adults that inherit the defences, are well protected regardless of the quality of their food; not least, as some inferior plants will enable caterpillars to acquire only basic protection. Synthesising the toxins directly comes with a cost, however, because those caterpillars that must take this route use up a lot more energy and are less likely to survive.

The same animal in different life stages, such as the caterpillar and adult of the six-spot burnet moth in the UK, can use varied colours as warning signals.

BEHIND THE SCIENCE

It doesn't take long to notice a familiar theme in the costumes of land animals with warning colours. From the skins of poison frogs to the wing cases of a ladybird, colours such as red, yellow and black dominate over blues, browns, greens and ultraviolet. A number of reasons may explain this. To begin with, the foliage of forests, grasslands, and many other habitats tends towards green, with the ground below grey or brown. One of the chief aims of any warning signal is to stand out and be seen, and so red, yellow and orange jump out from the backdrop and are distinctive and visible. Taking this approach means that a protected animal can be detected from as far away as possible, such that a predator can abort an attack even before getting too close. The combination of black with yellow or red offers a high contrast within the pattern of the animal itself and against the environment. On the other hand, some warning patterns are not as visible as they could be, if, for example, an animal would rather not be seen in the first instance. Here, more muted colours may be preferable. In the oceans, where warning signals have probably existed for the longest, it's a little different. Here, the complex environment, not least of all a coral reef, tends to be vivid in itself, with an abundance of yellow and red corals. As a result, the warning signals used by many marine animals seem to be much more diverse in colour.

Another reason for the specific colours often found in warning signals is that those colours tend to be quite reliable over time. As the light conditions change during the day, or the dappled light in a forest comes and goes, red and yellow hues tend to remain a constant shade. This is important because it means that predators should be able to recognise the warning signal even as light conditions and weather change. It also appears that predators are better at learning and remembering the classic colours used in warning signals than other ones. There's something in the psychology of many terrestrial animals that they remember yellow prey better than blue. Certain predators, including birds, are wary of yellows and blacks, even if they have never seen those hues before. Add to this the fact that many warning signals comprise relatively simple patterns, such as the black and yellow striped abdomen of a wasp, which are easy to notice, as they stand out from the complex mosaic of vegetation.

Many mammalian grazers appear content to ingest a variety of grasses and weeds, but if there's one thing they should want to avoid in Europe, it's ragwort. These plants, which love to grow in run-down patches of land, are full of toxins; yet they attract insects, none more so than the caterpillars of cinnabar moths. The larvae are marked with the classic signs of a warning signal – yellow and black stripes – and acquire their defences from the ragwort. Yet cinnabar moth larvae also demonstrate how the colours of animals often perform more than one job.

Cinnabar caterpillars are not born with defences, so they must gain them from their food plants and become more protected as they feed and grow. Like many creatures with warning signals, they like one another's company, clustering together on the same plants, especially when young. These aggregations of defended prey, from caterpillars to stink bugs, are widely found in species with warning signals. It helps to enhance the vibrancy of the message to predators and lessens the chances that an enemy will take a chance, compared to a lone individual.

Cinnabar caterpillars share a feature with the poison dart frogs. They don't just rely on standing out, but on blending in as well. From afar, their yellow and black stripes merge together and so match the background. All animals, including humans, are limited in our ability to resolve patterns, called our sense of acuity. Some creatures have better acuity than others, such as an eagle that can spot a rabbit from high in the sky, compared to a fly that struggles to resolve patterns, even when up close. For all creatures, there comes a point whereby they are so far away from something that they cannot resolve the pattern any more, or the markings are just too small. This is much like how we can struggle to read the small letters at the opticians and would find it even harder were we to take a few steps back. The stripes on the caterpillars allow them to evade being seen from afar, since the yellow colour merges into the yellow of the flowers, and the

Camouflaged or conspicuous? Cinnabar moth caterpillars have markings that can blend in or stand out depending on how closely they are seen.

average coloration of the larvae from afar blends to look like the vegetation. Close up, however, the message is clear; in fact, as the larvae grow, the stripes get thicker and easier to see from further away, while the animal also becomes increasingly more toxic. As for the adults, they feed on ragwort nectar to top up their defences, but signal them not with yellow, but stunning red and black wings.

Grouping together is a common approach to enhancing the effectiveness of warning signals, and it is a strategy used not only by caterpillars but by many other insects besides. In the desert lands of Arizona, mesquite trees are well adapted to cope with the heat and dryness. Able to extract water from deep below the ground, and with thorny vegetation to deter herbivores, there is one insect that relies on it for food: the giant mesquite bug. These large insects, several centimetres long as adults, cluster together in their nymph stages, sucking sugar-rich liquid from the seed pods growing on the trees. Each animal is a stunning mixture of deep red, with white spots and black bands. As smaller nymphs, the bugs produce chemicals that are best suited to deter their main threats, other insects. Additionally, the combined effect of multiple individuals together makes for a striking visual scene, well suited to deter larger predators. The nymphs secrete an unpleasant liquid that not only tastes bad but also smells bad. The combined effect is a valuable way to fend off a variety of threats, and the chemical defences also work as an alarm signal for the group to disperse should they come under attack. By summer, the bugs have matured into adults that are much duller, but with a body more structurally reinforced with thicker exoskeleton to survive any attack from birds or lizards. Adults also produce different sorts of unpleasant chemicals, which are most effective at fending off vertebrates; the large size of the adults is defence enough against other insects.

Overleaf: Many insects with warning signals aggregate together to enhance their display, like these giant mesquite bugs from the USA.

BEHIND THE SCIENCE

Darwin need not have worried quite so much about the existence of colourful yet non-breeding animals, but there is an aspect to the evolution of warning signals that has been harder for scientists to explain – how they evolved in the first instance. The paradox is this: if warning signals require predators to have learnt what they mean in order to work, how did they arise and spread in the first place? We can imagine some historical point in time on Earth, when no animals had yet evolved warning signals, but some were perhaps starting to acquire toxic defences. None of the predators at this point would have learnt to recognise yellows, blacks, oranges and beyond as signs of danger. The first creatures to evolve warning signals would have been attacked by naïve predators on account of being highly visible, and perhaps snuffed out before the warning signal had a chance to spread through a population and begin to work, by which time at least some of the predators had learnt what they mean. Scientists have long been puzzled by this issue, but in fact, there are several solutions.

For one thing, many predators are not the reckless risk-takers that we assume they are. On the contrary, many animals tend to be neophobic; that is, they avoid things they have never seen before. So, a bright red caterpillar might simply be avoided through being new. Similarly, predators are often conservative in what they eat. Rather like how many of us might pick the same meal on a menu in a restaurant each time, predators often show the same reluctance to branch out. Part of the reason is that eating new things can expose you to risks – perhaps you might attempt to eat something that has gone off, tastes bad, or even is much harder to capture than first thought. Such responses can have a powerful influence on how predators respond to prey. As it happens, many of the defences that animals have, including poisons, not only make the predator sick but also smell and taste bad. This is almost certainly no coincidence – it's better to stop a predator early on than to risk being eaten, in order for the foe to learn how bad you are.

Another solution to the problem is that a variety of poisonous animals have physical defences too. Many caterpillars, such as those of the peacock butterfly, are covered with irritating hairs or spines, not something that would be pleasant to touch, let alone eat. Beyond this, the bodies of many insects marked with warnings are often reinforced with tougher exoskeletons, meaning that even if they are attacked, they have a chance to survive. Finally, a great many creatures that use warning displays live in groups. These aggregations tend to be animals from the same brood and hence are siblings sharing many of the same genes. If one or two of them get picked off by predators, the enemies still learn and enough of the prey survive to spread the new defence. So, while evolving warning signals was clearly a risk, there is a host of reasons as to how seemingly suicidal defences like these evolved in the first place.

The premise of a warning display is that it is honest, and both the predator and prey benefit from it. The prey animal keeps its life, while the predator avoids a nasty meal or even harm to itself. For some animals, bright colours are used to buy time, causing the predator to pause and so give the potential victim time to flee – a defence called a startle display. Some of the most wonderful demonstrations of this come from the so-called underwing, or *Catocala*, moths. There are many species of these medium-sized denizens of the night, which make a perfectly safe and tasty meal for predators, but all have forewings that are wonderfully camouflaged in the trees and other vegetation, where they hide during the day. The forewings cover up a bright costume, for the hindwings are painted with reds, oranges, yellows, blues, blacks and more hues besides. The exact colours and patterning differ among species, but the function is to make a predatory bird or lizard pause its attack.

When threatened, the moth will move its forewings and expose the bright underwings. On encountering such a dramatic change, the predator, if all goes to plan for the insect, will pause or even abandon the attack, allowing the moth time to fly off and hide elsewhere. The question is, why do so many varieties of hindwing colours exist? The problem for any startle display is that, if seen often enough, a predator starts to ignore it. After all, if a red flash is never followed by a nasty experience, a bird can start to disregard it and eat the moth instead. However, if each time the bird sees a new colour – first blue, then red, followed by yellow, and so on – then it is constantly on a state of alert and never knows what's coming next. The opportunity to become accustomed to the same colour is much lower, and the constant appearance of something novel always comes with the risk that potential harm may be present. Thus, each type of moth benefits because, in the whole community of species and individuals, their own colour type is just one of many.

Other moths use a similar, yet subtle variation on startle displays for protection. The garden tiger moth is a stunningly marked insect, with black and cream zebra-like forewings and bright orange hindwings with black spots. It is active during the day, but when disturbed darts for cover. The moth, when flying, is a blur of orange and black, something bright and vivid to draw a predator's attention. So, when a tiger moth plunges into

Jersey tiger moths on the island of Rhodes, Greece, gather in large numbers. They only display their bright hind wings when needed for defence.

Overleaf: Not all deterrents in nature rely on the same colours. Lantern bugs (top left), blue-winged grasshoppers (bottom left), garden tiger moths (top right) and mountain katydids (bottom right) utilise a variety of hues.

the vegetation, a hungry bird is left looking for something orange, rather than the inconspicuous black and white creature that now presents itself, and the moth may go unnoticed. This is called a flash display and is common in critters like grasshoppers, which frequently have brightly coloured legs and wings. When they jump and fly, an antagonist is drawn to the bright yellows or blues, but as soon as they stop the grasshoppers blend in perfectly with the grey and brown environment. The predator is left searching for something colourful, but misses the creature in its new disguise.

Tiger moths are not, in fact, reliant only on flash displays and camouflage for defence. They also have toxins accumulated in their bodies and the orange colours act as a classic warning signal. This is true not just for the garden tiger, but a host of other tiger moth species. And, many of those moths are keen to use their warning signals as a back-up, should the predator get too close. Wood tiger moths, a species found across Palaearctic

regions, seem reluctant to reveal their bright red or orange hindwings, and only when a predator is really bothering them, backed up by unpleasant-tasting body fluids that they secrete. In this species, the hindwing costume can vary. Males come in two types: those with yellow hindwings and those where the wings are white. Initially, this seems rather puzzling, because varying the appearance of the warning signal means that predators have more types to learn to avoid, potentially increasing the risk to the moths. Furthermore, the moths with yellow wings are less likely to be attacked by birds, and they have higher survival chances in the wild. So why have white wings at all? Rather like the poison frogs, colour often serves multiple functions, and it turns out that males with white wings are more attractive to females than those with yellow. It's a trade-off, between staying alive and securing a mate.

Defensive adverts that are only switched on as needed, perhaps for maximum effect, are also found rather extravagantly in a katydid (bush cricket). The mountain katydid, found in Australia's alpine regions, is well defended, but primarily relies on camouflage to avoid attracting unwanted attention, especially from birds such as Australian magpies. When at risk, a katydid lifts its wings to reveal stunning colours over its abdomen: a banding of red, blue and black. The effect is to stun and cause the bird to pause, as in a startle display, and, at the same time, to teach any persistent animal that it doesn't taste nice either. Strangely, the insect only reveals its defence as a last resort, when it is physically pecked. Quite why it waits so long and how risky this is, remains to be seen.

* * *

BEHIND THE SCIENCE

It is a rather curious fact that many animals with warning signals are quite variable in appearance. From poison frogs to tiger moths, individuals of the same species often look dissimilar in patterning and coloration. This poses a problem because, for warning colours to work, the predators must either have some inbuilt wariness of bright hues, or they must learn to avoid warning-coloured prey through negative experiences, not least feeling the ill effects of consuming a toxic animal. Yet if individuals vary in colour, it means that the predators must learn to avoid not one but multiple colour forms, and, in turn, the risk of attacks on each prey animal is higher, from naïve predators that have not learnt about their costume.

In truth, scientists still struggle to understand why this phenomenon is so common, but there are several explanations. Some of these are rather complex and relate to how the behaviour of predators can change depending on the time of year, the animal's geographical range and the abundance of other prey sources. Some predators may also be better at generalising one prey type to another, such that a negative encounter with a yellow moth will make them also wary of similar-looking moths, but which are coloured orange. Other explanations are easier to appreciate, especially those in which the colour of an animal must perform several tasks. As with the poison frogs, cinnabar larvae and wood tiger moths, different selection pressures on the coloration of an animal exist. An animal's ultimate colour may be the combined outcome of having to avoid attack, attract a mate, thermoregulate and more besides. This need to satisfy many functions can drive variation among animals.

It's hard to get most people excited about slugs, but beneath the waves are slugs of a very different kind from those we see in the garden, and they wear some of the most vibrant and extravagant badges found anywhere in nature. Not only that, but there are thousands of species throughout the world's oceans, and they range in size from just a few millimetres to more than 70 centimetres long. The largest, the California black sea hare, can weigh in excess of 10 kilograms. Some of the most colourful are called nudibranchs, meaning 'open gills', for many species have feathery gill-like projections extending from their backs that obtain oxygen from the water. These creatures, of which 3,000 species are known, have done away with any form of internal shell in their adult lives and instead rely on other defences. Nudibranchs are the darlings of many divers and those beachcombers lucky enough to find them in rock pools. They certainly would not attack garden plants, since nudibranchs are strictly carnivorous.

Sea slugs are colourful for a reason: they pack an arsenal of defences that render them a meal best avoided by hungry fish. Some of the most incredible things about sea slugs are both how they get their defences and the range of weaponry that they have at their disposal.

In Australia, around islands and shallow waters off Queensland's coastline, coral reefs dot the seabed, patrolled by dazzling fish darting in and out of the corals. For a tiny sea slug, this is a dangerous world. Owing to the mixing of relatively warm tropical and cool temperate waters, an abundance of different niches and many different food sources, diversity of sea slugs is high here. In fact, there are over 300 known species in this area.

Sea slugs are experts at attacking and eating things that most other creatures would be foolish to touch. Many species love to feast on small hydroids, the stinging relatives of jellyfish that often grow on seaweed and rocks and sea anemones, which also normally have a powerful sting. One nudibranch, called the blue dragon, found in the surface waters of the open ocean, even specialises in eating colonial hydroids, such as the infamous Portuguese man o' war, attacking them with sharp teeth. These particular sea slugs use gas chambers to float along in the ocean currents, hoping to bump into their prey. They are not just protected against the defences of their food, but actively consume the stinging cells and incorporate them into their own bodies. The backs of many nudibranchs are covered with finger-like projections, called cerata, and into these cerata the animal adds in the still-active stinging cells of its meal. Not only does it get dinner, but the nudibranch gets a potent defence. It is even capable of giving humans a nasty sting. The blue dragon highlights it with stunning colours – electric blue stripes and circles.

Marine sea slugs use some of the most extravagant costumes in nature, such as this yellow skirt sea slug from Cornwall, UK.

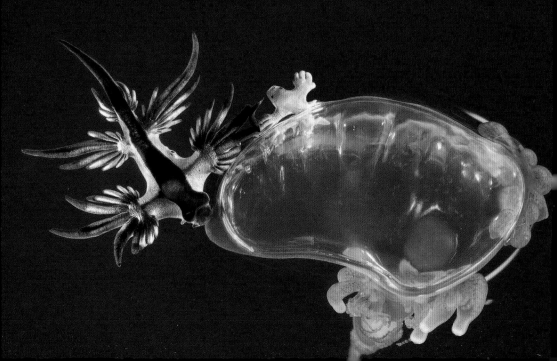

Other species of sea slug consume things like sponges and again synthesise powerful toxins into their body from their food. In the case of nudibranchs, and many sea slugs generally, the hunted has become the hunter. They have small eyes and poor vision, and so finding their prey is achieved with chemical sensors. Studies of the appearance and toxicity of sea slugs from Queensland show that species which are more vibrant and contrast more strongly with the background tend to carry defences that should be more harmful to predators. This reaffirms that many warning displays don't just tell a predator that an animal is defended, but also reveal just how defended the bearer is.

In the UK, there exists a surprisingly large number of sea slugs, many of them under-reported and scarcely seen, except by those who know exactly where and how to find them in rock pools or when diving. It's partly because many are small or found in deeper water, but also because even marine scientists haven't searched that much for them, at least until recently. But UK species are often astonishing in coloration and behaviour too. One of the most impressive species is the grey sea slug, which can reach 15 centimetres and feeds on sea anemones, especially the snakelocks. These beautiful anemones come in either a brown form or a vibrant glowing green, with purple-tipped tentacles, and pack a potent defence. The grey sea slug takes the stinging cells of the anemone and moves them into the mass of cerata projecting from its back. The colour of grey sea slugs is not always grey – in fact, they can be brown or rose coloured, depending on the colour of the anemone they have most recently devoured. Another broadly similar-looking species, *Aeolidiella alderi*, favours daisy anemones, for much the same reason. Other species of sea slug in the UK use differing defences. The yellow-plumed sea slug, a translucent yellow blob, secretes sulphuric acid if threatened, as does a warty-looking sea

The nudibranchs **Hypselodoris infucata** *from Java (top left) and* **Flabellina nobilis** *from the Atlantic Ocean (top right) show striking diversity in warning coloration. Many nudibranchs obtain potent defences from their diet, like the pelagic blue dragon (bottom), which reuses the stinging cells from the Portuguese man o' war that it eats.*

slug called *Geitodoris planata*. One of the UK's most striking species, *Polycera quadrilineata* feeds on bryozoan mats that encrust kelp and other seaweed, turning parts of its meal into internal toxins, which it advertises with yellow and black markings. Other species, like *Facelina auriculata*, are bright pink-purple, or, as with the orange-clubbed sea slug, have projections that are striking orange in hue. So, while garden slugs may be difficult to love, their marine counterparts are a world apart.

***

Much variation exists in the strength of animal toxins, and in some cases super-strength defences are needed because predators have evolved the wherewithal to overcome weaker toxins. The rough-skinned newt is an amphibian native to North America. The top side of its body is dark brown, not particularly colourful, but, when disturbed, it curls up its head and tail to show off a bright orange belly. Like the poison frogs, the newt produces a

The nudibranch Facelina auriculata *searches for small hydroids to eat. This is a relatively common species in the UK.*

toxic defence excreted from its skin, the deadly tetrodotoxin again. The newt is attacked by garter snakes, and the predators have, remarkably, evolved a nervous system with cells that are resistant to the effects of tetrodotoxin. So, the newt must up its game and produce higher strength poison if it is to have the desired effect. The cost, however, is that tetrodotoxin is not cheap to produce, and the newt must expend valuable energy making it, which would otherwise be allocated for reproduction or moving around its habitat.

* * *

Not all animals with warning colours are conveying the fact that they are toxic to ingest. A great variety of creatures use coloration to warn that they have a venomous bite. No country on the planet has quite the reputation of Australia as home to such a large number of potentially deadly creatures, and those living in its coastal waters are no exception. Australia's coastlines are inhabited

The yellow-orange belly and throat of a rough-skinned newt –
a sign predators should think twice before attacking.

by some of the ocean's most colourful creatures, and many of them display just how dangerous they are. A competition for the world's most venomous animal inevitably includes the blue-ringed octopus. Found all over the Indo-Pacific region, but especially Australia, it resides in rock pools, cracks and crevices on the shallow reef. When undisturbed, it looks like any other octopus, but, when aggravated, it changes dramatically.

Like all octopuses, it is venomous, capable of injecting poison into other animals. Often, this is used in feeding, where the octopus first uses its beak to break the skin or shell of its victim, before it injects the toxins, particularly when hunting crabs, other crustaceans and fish. In doing this, the octopus paralyses its prey, so that it can feed with the victim subdued. In other instances, it uses its venom as a defence. Although other octopuses have this security, the poison of the blue-ringed is far more potent than any other or, indeed, most poisons known to humans. The venom a single animal possesses is apparently capable of killing several dozen people, not that the animal has any desire to, and bites to humans are almost unknown. Its venom, produced in the saliva glands, is tetrodotoxin – the same poison found in some puffer fish – and it works by blocking nerve impulses. It is thought to be a thousand times more deadly than cyanide.

In spite of its defence, the blue-ringed octopus is undoubtedly at risk of being seen as a good meal by a variety of reef animals. Its body is just a few centimetres long, and, even with the arms, it still comes to about 15 centimetres and weighs little over 20 grams. Octopuses make tasty meals for many predators, and one this size is a manageable bite size. When threatened, however, the blue-ringed octopus changes from being relatively inconspicuous to displaying the stunning electric blue rings that give the species its name. Within one second, 50 or 60 rings appear and pulsate. Like other octopuses, special chromatophore cells in its

The striking markings on a venomous blue-ringed octopus stand out against the background in waters off West Papua, Indonesia.

skin contract or expand to quickly change the distribution of pigments across its body, and these help to change its appearance. Underneath is another special type of cell: iridophores, which reflects blue-green and ultraviolet light. A further cell type, called leucophores, broadly reflects lots of light back, more like a mirror, to add brightness to the display. The combination of these cells, and the nerve cells that control them, enables the blue rings to appear lightning fast and dazzle in brightness.

There are suggestions that there may be more than ten species of blue-ringed octopus, rather than just the handful described at the moment. Different species seem to have distinctive rings, and they may even use them to communicate with one another. Regardless, blue is a good choice of colour for these marine animals since, in shallow coastal waters, blue-green light is abundant and many of the potential predators, such as fish, can see well in this part of the spectrum. Quite why the octopus

needs such potent venom is not clear. Like the infamous black widow spider or a black mamba snake, many of the most venomous creatures have far more potent venom than would be needed to kill an attacker or, for that matter, their prey. Perhaps the super strength enables the venom to work more quickly, incapacitating the enemy before it can do any real harm.

* * *

In the deserts and scrubland of the southern USA and northern Mexico lives a striking lizard, notable not only for its appearance but also for being one of only a handful of lizards worldwide capable of producing venom. The Gila monster is unmistakable, with bright orange or yellow coloration in bands and blotches, set against a dark brown or black body.

It has long been known that Gila monsters have a bite that carries an extra kick. They produce venom in modified saliva glands, and the toxin is added into the victim via the mouth when biting. The venom runs along groves in the teeth and is often chewed into the wound more deeply for extra effect. It is a moderately potent neurotoxin, capable of producing extreme pain. However, the bite is almost never fatal to humans and much less venom is produced than by other creatures, such as snakes. That said, the bite on its own can be rather substantial, with sharp teeth and a powerful grip, often accompanied by a firm reluctance to let go.

Possessing warning signals can sometimes enable animals to more brazenly go about their business, such as this Gila monster out in the open.

Gila monsters are not especially agile. In fact, lethargic would be a much fairer description. They spend most of their lives hiding in crevices, burrows and under rocks, venturing out mostly early and late in the day. When they do head into the wider world they are often seen climbing about looking for birds eggs to eat. Only about 10 per cent of the time are they exposed and in the open, but their warning signals during such times are unmistakable. A sign to which careless coyotes and raptors should pay attention. The slow nature of the lizards probably explains why they needed to evolve other defences.

* * *

An assortment of snakes, even very venomous ones, tend to rely primarily on camouflage to avoid being eaten, but all is not always what it seems. There are striking exceptions. The most colourful of these are the coral snakes. This varied and widespread group comprises species that are known to have a venomous bite with toxins that affect the respiratory system. Many snakes that are harmless have evolved to look like coral snakes that live in the same neighbourhood, so that they too are protected from attack, leading to various versions of the popular rhyme: 'Red on yellow, kill a fellow; red on black, venom lack'. This refers to the arrangement of the banding pattern on these snakes, whereby the sequence of red, yellow and black bands is not precisely matched in the harmless snakes. However, it is far from perfect, since many coral snakes vary in colour, and some even lack clear banding.

Other venomous serpents lack the bright colours of coral snakes, but instead highlight their defence with characteristic patterning. The European adder is Britain's only venomous snake. As far as its potency is concerned, it is a long way off the

Different ways to stand out – the European adder (top) has muted but distinctive zig-zag markings, whereas the aquatic coral snake from Ecuador uses conspicuous colour bands to warn others.

most dangerous species. Its mild venom is primarily used to subdue small mammals, lizards and bird nestlings, which it hunts in the heathland and woodland habitats that it favours. When at risk, it slinks off into the vegetation. Its bite, though, can be painful for large animals, including us, if we are unlucky enough to have a close encounter.

Across their range, adders are also hunted by predators of their own, principally birds of prey. The grey-brown colour of most adders is marked prominently with a black zig-zag pattern down the snake's back. To human eyes, the snakes don't look especially visible, perhaps even well matched to their environment, rather like cinnabar moth larvae when seen from afar. Scientists have often wondered if the markings are a type of camouflage. However, zig-zag patterns are common in viper species, and they are certainly distinctive. Like most snakes, adders and other similar vipers would much rather flee or hide than be forced to defend themselves, but they can put themselves at risk of attack when basking in the open, absorbing the sun's rays. Their patterns, however, warn predators not to take the risk.

The Coto Doñana National Park in southern Spain is famous for its wetland reserves and abundance and diversity of bird species. The habitat and wider area beyond, besides the wetlands, is a mixture of scrub bushes, sand dunes and pine trees. It's the perfect habitat for snakes, and in its open spaces many species can be seen basking and lying in wait for prey. One is the snub-nosed adder, a snake with a grey-brown body adorned with beautiful chocolate- and black-coloured zig-zag patterns. Other species, which are non-venomous, also live in the area, and they are often targeted by birds of prey, including common buzzard, short-toed eagle, booted eagle and black kites. Snakes that lack the prominent zig-zags, and are either generally camouflaged or marked with stripes or less pronounced patterns, are attacked frequently by the birds, but the warning patterns of the snub-nosed adder ensure that it is avoided. Enemies have learnt that there are less risky meals to be had elsewhere.

In parts of Asia lives the tiger keelback snake. It's a striking animal, which in some locations is marked with yellow and black patterns, or white and black markings elsewhere, and even with red in some localities. Keelbacks feast on amphibians, many of which are well protected themselves, including some of the snake's favourite quarry: frogs and toads. The poison secreted by toxic toads of the genus *Bufo* does not protect them from the snake, which is actively looking for the toad; in fact, the snake sequesters the poison and stores it in special body glands found just behind the head, so these snakes are both venomous and poisonous. Like many other snakes, keelbacks are at risk of attack from snake-eating hawks, yet when threatened, the keelback can flatten its body to show off its warnings to the bird. Why the snakes vary in coloration across populations, and whether there is any link to how well defended they are, remains to be understood. However, remarkably, the snakes appear to be aware of whether they have toxic defences or not. Those found in parts of Japan where they can feast on toads will perform the characteristic threat displays, whereas snakes living on islands lacking toads will turn and flee instead.

As a further use of their defence, mother snakes pass on some of the toxins they have acquired to their offspring, so that the young are protected even as they hatch out from their eggs. The bright yellow or white banding patterns around the neck of juveniles may also serve as a warning to animals that might try to attack.

***

Some species of fish have venom too. It is used in defence and injected into an attacker by means of modified fins and spines. The most well-known of these fish are the lionfish. They are stunning to look at, with the dangerous venom signalled through elaborate spines radiating from the body, covered with a mixture of contrasting brown-red and white markings. Few predators are brave or experienced enough to tackle a lionfish and come out on top. Sadly, lionfish are also ferocious predators themselves, and they have become an invasive species, moving out of their more usual haunts in the Indo-Pacific region to cause mayhem in the Caribbean, off Florida and in the Mediterranean. With so many predators put off by their bright colours and sharp spines, and so few creatures able to eat lionfish, they have been upsetting ecosystems in many marine environments. A variety of control measures is in place to reduce their numbers, but owing to their serious defences, people have to be well trained before taking part, else they end up hurting themselves.

While many animals rely on internal poisons, and others on a venomous bite, a few creatures adopt rather more unpleasant protective measures. Furthermore, instead of relying on red, yellow and orange, these animals take a more monochromatic approach. Few animals come with a smellier reputation than the skunk. Found widely in North America, this medium-sized mammal is hard to misidentify, with its bushy tail and black body with white stripes. Although darker and muted shades are often thought of as most useful in concealment, black and white offer high visual contrast, not least in gloomy forests and around dawn and dusk. For skunks, their markings warn potential aggressors that they shouldn't mess with them. When threatened, a skunk will raise its tail and arch its back, claw the ground, and then even charge, if it continues to be provoked. Should that fail, it will spray a jet of noxious liquid from its anal gland, which can be propelled up to a distance of 4 metres. This is genuinely not nice: besides its awful odour, it can cause sickness and even temporarily blind the aggressor.

The effectiveness of skunk defences has been well studied in places such as California. Here, predators are hesitant to approach the black and white coloration of skunks, and their level of caution is higher when there are more skunks in the neighbourhood. Bad experiences in the past heighten their sense of wariness. Skunks, in principle, could be attacked by predators such coyotes, foxes, bobcats, mountain lions and black bears, but they're not. While experienced predators avoid them, young and naïve foes may not yet have learnt to steer clear and end up with a nasty surprise. The white stripes are a clear warning, even to enemies, such as the many mammals that have poor colour vision, and the orientation of the markings is even said to direct the gaze of the attacker to the site where the liquid jets out.

Lionfish are well protected from predators and signal it with their characteristic patterns, part of the reason for them being so invasive across the world.

Skunks are by far the most widely known black and white mammal to pack a defence. But they are not alone, and similar markings and protection have independently evolved in other mammals. One such species is the zorilla, an African weasel that is also covered in fur with black and white stripes. Like skunks, zorillas spray toxic liquid at enemies, and they also warn predators by initially arching their back and raising their tail. It takes time and energy to make the defensive fluid, so it's better to avoid using it, unless really needed. The foul-smelling substance is produced from anal stink glands and causes burning and temporary blindness. These two creatures, the skunk and the zorilla, are a wonderful example of convergent evolution, whereby two distantly related organisms separately evolve a similar appearance or way of life, rather like features of flight and wing form in extinct pterosaurs and modern-day bats. A variety of other small-to-medium sized black and white mammals also exist, from wolverines and badgers to polecats, and in many cases their coloration acts as a sign of danger too; but not of toxic spray, but instead of being ferocious and something not worth attacking.

The ferocious honey badger – more than a match for most predators.

The honey badger is perhaps the most notorious of such animals, fervently fighting back against iconic predators such as lions.

**

Nature is nothing if not diverse, and warning signals perhaps illustrate that as well as any type of adaptation. The diversity of colours and patterns used, the varied accompanying behaviours, the multiplicative ways that the creatures derive their defences and how they work all showcase nature's variety. Warning signals are a perilous approach because the animal risks being seen, and, to combat that, some animals use it as a last resort, or hold back when they are most visible. Alternatively, they live in groups where they might be less of a target, or adopt some of the most potent chemicals known to humankind, such that if they are attacked, the aggressor is quickly incapacitated. For other creatures, the risks are too great and over evolution they have taken a very different route to survival: they hide in plain sight.

An African zorilla from Namibia; like skunks, it is capable of squirting noxious chemicals when under threat.

CHAPTER FIVE

CAMOUFLAGE

Clinging to a brightly coloured sea fan in the tropical
waters of the Indo-Pacific, a tiny animal just
2 centimetres long is at great risk of ending up as a
meal for patrolling predators. It is a seahorse, and is
arguably the most charismatic of these endearing
animals: a pygmy seahorse.

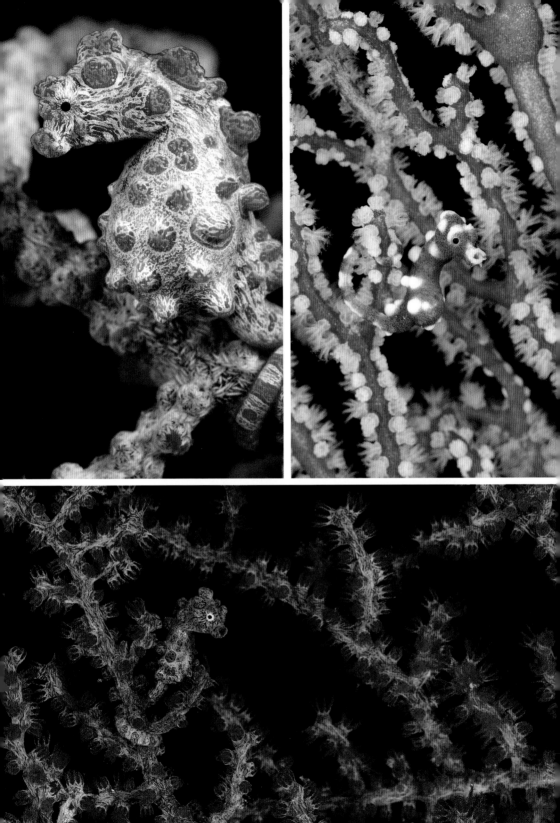

Not much is known about the biology of these animals, though there are at least seven known species. They are the darlings of divers and underwater photographers – if they can be found, that is. In their natural environment, these fish blend in spectacularly well with the corals, taking on orange, pink, red and a variety of other hues to match the colour of the specific fan on which they live. Little bumps on their body, called tubercles, create texture to further enhance the resemblance to their home. The seahorses start life as a dull brown or grey colour, but once they find a suitable fan to live on, they change to match it exquisitely well.

Of all the uses of colour in nature, few have provided such compelling evidence of natural selection as the breath-taking camouflage of a great variety of animals. The exquisite match between a plethora of creatures and their environments is testament to the vital need to hide, both for predators and prey. The sometimes scarcely believable matches arise through a variety of means, from changes occurring in populations over thousands of years, to individual creatures being able to morph their appearance in the blink of an eye. The approaches and colour forms taken are as varied as they are impressive, but, camouflage does not only rely on blending in and broadly matching the colour and pattern of the environment; it works in a wondrous diversity of ways.

✳ ✳ ✳

In a sub-Saharan forest, a West African Gaboon viper lies in wait. On its body, the pattern of squares and diamonds merges with the light and dark patches in the leaf litter. The markings on its trunk, a mixture of yellows, browns and blacks, are also arranged in such a way as to create an optical illusion of many disconnected

Tiny, colourful, but exquisitely camouflaged, pygmy seahorses hide in the safety of sea fans in Indonesia.

objects, rather than the body of a snake. The viper uses its camouflage to ambush unsuspecting prey, while also hiding from threats to itself.

The snake's impressive camouflage is made even more effective by a special optical trick. Microscopic leaf-like structures in the skin trap light, making the viper's black markings another example of 'super-black' in nature. The dark patterns give added depth, allowing parts of the serpent's body to merge with the shadows. As we have seen, super-black is found in the mating colours of butterflies and birds-of-paradise, when it is used to enhance the vibrancy of other hues, but the viper shows it can also be an effective way to hide; in fact, this approach is used to an even greater extent by some deep-sea fish. In the dark depths of the ocean's midnight zone, many predators hunt with bioluminescent searchlights. To hide, an animal must disappear into the blackness, but bioluminescent torches pose a problem. One solution is to

The colour of a tiger's coat can help camouflage its body. The deer on which it preys are unable to distinguish between red, orange and green, such that, to a deer, an orange tiger can blend into green grass. Here, we have our view of a tiger compared to a deer's view.

use skin made super-black by tiny nanostructures, which are structures too small to see with a microscope. They suck up all the light that falls on the bearer so that, even if the fish comes under the searchlights of a predator, they still cannot be seen in the darkness.

✳ ✳ ✳

Few animals are as iconic as the Bengal tiger. One mention of that name instantly conjures images of their regal orange colour and black stripes. They live in the grasslands and dry forests of India, Bangladesh and Nepal, where they hunt deer, wild boar and other mammals. Like any relationship between predator and prey, evolution has shaped each to excel at survival. The tiger is an expert hunter – agile, stealthy and equipped with sensitive night vision, smell and hearing, while its prey is constantly alert to danger, quick and well hidden. Tigers, though, are ambush predators. Like most other big cats, they don't chase down prey over long distances; that's behaviour more often found in packs of wild dogs. A 250-kilogram tiger can't run at speed for long; instead, it creeps up on its quarry, slowly getting closer and closer until it can strike with a burst of power and a killing bite to the neck. The problem for the tiger is to be able to move close enough without being seen, which isn't easy given their huge size.

To us, the orange and black colours of a tiger are instantly recognisable. After all, few other large creatures in the terrestrial world have such a striking colour pattern, but the deer, and the many other animals that tigers hunt, lack our sense of colour perception. They can't tell the difference between oranges, yellows and greens. To a deer, the tiger's orange and black stripes blend in perfectly to the greens and browns of the grassland and forest. The tiger sports a coat of camouflage that renders it difficult to spot, but deer have eyes capable of detecting movement all around them, along with other keen senses, especially hearing, so, even with such effective camouflage, less than 10 per cent of tiger hunts are successful. Quite why the tiger's fur is orange, rather than the brown colours seen in most other large mammals, is a bit of a mystery, since it lacks good colour vision. Even though the tiger's coat makes specific use of the colour orange, it is still a striking example of how camouflage in nature needs to match the wider environment, not to us, but to the eyes of those at which the costume is directed.

* * *

Camouflage is by no means used solely for attack. As the pygmy seahorse demonstrates, it is much more widely employed as a means of defence; after all, while the risk of being seen by potential prey may mean a lost meal for a predator, being spotted by a predator may mean death for the prey. The selection pressure to be hidden is generally stronger for those under attack than for those doing the hunting. Blending into the background using special markings and colours is also just one trick that many creatures use. Some animals have defences that are less obvious, but very effective.

Sitting on a leaf in the jungles of Panama, a small frog remains motionless. Seen from afar, its body is light green, but a closer inspection reveals that the animal is partly transparent. When inspected from below, many of the creature's internal organs can been seen inside its small frame. This is a glass frog, and, perhaps as expected, the combination of green skin and translucent body helps it to blend in with the leafy environment in which it lives.

Unlike many animals that are almost fully transparent, such as juvenile eels and glass shrimp, the glass frog is only partially see-through. Its legs are relatively translucent, but the body itself, when seen from above, is largely pale green. Making an entire body fully transparent is challenging. For a start, the animal's flesh and organs have to be modified to work with the optics of the environment in order to allow light through, without crucial body functions being compromised. Some parts of the body, notably the eyes and certain internal organs, simply cannot work as transparent tissue. We might wonder then, why the frog does not simply have skin that is fully leaf-green. The answer is that foliage is not just one shade of green. It varies, with some leaves greener or brighter than others; so, the moment a bright lime-green frog hops from a pale to a dark leaf, it will be easy to see.

The glass frog's solution is to allow some of the light from the leaf below it to pass through its body, specifically the legs and margins of the main trunk. By doing this, it helps the animal to match the hue and brightness of the leaf below, and the edges and limbs of its body to blend in more effectively. The margins of the frog, in particular, lose their distinct shape and blend in better, hiding the outline of the amphibian from the watchful eyes of avian predators.

Glass frogs are not the only animals to utilise transparency. The strategy is also found in butterflies and moths. Several of these creatures do not rely solely on camouflage, but instead resemble other insects such as wasps or bees, or even toxic butterflies, whereby they couple yellow and black body colours with see-through wings. However, some of these insects, notably glasswing or clearwing butterflies, apparently also benefit from being see-through because it reduces the chances that they will be detected by hungry birds. These butterflies, which in certain cases also defend themselves with toxins, have wings that, aside from markings around the edges, are completely transparent. Chitin, which is used to make insect wings, is naturally transparent, so by avoiding the use of scales and pigments, the butterflies can make their wings see-through. Predatory birds are less likely to see species of clearwing butterflies when their degree of transparency is better. Beyond glass frogs and glasswing butterflies, transparency is really the dominion of aquatic animals, where the optics of water allow this form of defence to work more effectively, and it is prevalent in animals from glass catfish to certain squid.

The see-through disguise of Valerio's glass frog underneath a leaf in Costa Rica. The outline of the body blends in with the background showing through.

BEHIND THE SCIENCE

The Gaboon viper and tiger exemplify perhaps the most common type of camouflage, something called 'background matching'. Here, the colour and patterns on an animal have evolved to blend into the general background, such that the bearer goes unnoticed by prying eyes. Other creatures may be looking in the right direction, but fail to spot the concealed individual. This method of concealment is not perfect, however, and naturalists and scientists as long ago as the late 1800s realised that it has a crucial flaw: the body shape or outline is often still easy to discern, simply because it doesn't blend in perfectly with the immediate surroundings. Tell-tale features such as body edges, or even the eyes of an animal, can give its presence away. To combat this, many animals adopt high-contrast patterns, often placed at the body margins, some of which blend into the environment, alongside others that don't. The effect is to break up the appearance of shape and form, hiding the animal more effectively: a strategy called 'disruptive coloration'. Such markings are abundant on the wings of moths, such as the lime hawk moth, with its deep green markings set into otherwise pale pink wings. Across the natural world, creatures from fish to frogs also tend to have dark bands running across their eyes and head, the idea being to reduce the salience of the eyes, which might otherwise stand out.

A further challenge faced by many animals is that light from the sun comes from above, creating more intense lighting on the upper surface of the animal, and creating a shadow on its underside. Many visual systems utilise information from lighting and shading in nature to work out features of object shape and size, and the contrast created by shadows can therefore highlight the three-dimensional forms of many objects. To thwart this, an abundance of creatures use countershading, whereby those body parts facing stronger lighting are darker in colour, whereas their undersides are paler. Countershading is widely used in the marine world, not least on the bodies of sharks and bony fish. In fact, in this realm it has a double benefit – creatures looking down from above, towards the gloomy depths, don't see the dark topside of the animal swimming below, whereas those looking up might fail to see the pale silhouette against the sky above them.

Camouflage can be taken to even greater extremes. Many prawns and fish, for example, are transparent, such that the picture they present is one of the world immediately behind them. Thanks to the optics of the marine environment, transparency tends to work better under water than on land, though glass frogs and clearwing butterflies are notable exceptions. Other animals don't attempt to resemble the broader environment, but instead match specific objects. The early instars of an alder moth caterpillar are the spitting image of a bird dropping, as are many spiders, and a suite of insects pass off easily as sticks. The potoo birds from Central and South America, being much bigger animals, pretend to be a broken stump of a tree branch. They keep up this front when under threat, sneaking a watchful look out through tiny gaps in their otherwise closed eyes. Resembling objects in the environment, appropriately called 'masquerade', doesn't stop the animal from being seen, but instead an enemy mistakes the animal for something else – it fails to recognise the true identity of the individual that is hiding.

For most animals, especially terrestrial ones, allowing light to pass right through their bodies is not achievable. The costs of modifying their tissues is just too great, except, for instance, when the body tissue is naturally see-through, as with insect wings. This might explain why transparency is uncommon on land, and, even when it does exist, it is far from perfect, such as with glass frogs. In water, the optics of the environment make this an easier strategy to achieve. Transparency is also more common in smaller animals, including the juvenile life stages of many fish, because these animals, perhaps, are under greater risk of attack. The effects of light, though, can be mitigated in other ways.

* * *

The eyed hawk-moth caterpillar is an impressive beast, up to 7 centimetres in size, and a regular find on apple trees; that is, if it doesn't escape detection. Habitually, the caterpillar clings to the bottom of branches and leaves with its underside, which is darker, pointing at the sky. Being a big insect, and essentially a cylindrical shape, sunlight poses a problem because the surface of the animal facing up will cast a shadow on the side facing the ground. To rectify this, the caterpillar uses countershading, cancelling out the differences in lighting that would otherwise reveal its shape.

Many ocean creatures also rely on countershading, as differences in lighting can be more extreme under water. Countershading pigments can go only so far, however. The lighter bellies of many creatures can help the animal to hide from a predator lurking in the depths looking up, but it is hard to completely hide a silhouette this way. Some marine creatures have another trick to combat this.

In the deep waters of the northeastern Atlantic, sometimes down as far as 2,000 metres, lives an endearing fish, the velvet

Glasswing butterflies are a rare example of terrestrial animals that achieve exceptional levels of transparency, at least for parts of their body.

Invisibility in marine invertebrates, including this shrimp from the Great Barrier Reef, is achieved through almost complete transparency.

belly lanternshark. Growing to less than 50 centimetres long, it is hardly likely to draw comparisons with the Hollywood shark from the film *Jaws*, but it is a good-sized meal for many larger predators. It is also an abundant species, sometimes occurring in small shoals. Like other lanternsharks, individuals create light on their undersides that matches the faint glow from the surface above, called 'counter-illumination'. Their skin is packed with cells called photophores that produce bioluminescent light, just like the emissions seen in a range of creatures from fireflies to anglerfish, but here the use is not in attracting mates or food, but to hide. The use of such a cloaking mechanism can be highly refined, with light production varying with the conditions above. If the animal is closer to the surface, it must emit more light from its belly than when in deeper water. Counter-illumination is common in a variety of marine animals, not just sharks, but also bony fish and squid; in fact, fossil evidence

Upside down but still well hidden, this eyed hawk-moth caterpillar relies on its countershading.

suggested that counter-illumination in sharks reaches back to at least the Cretaceous period in Earth's history.

* * *

A tasty meal for a variety of animals, from seals and dolphins to sea bass and sharks, the European common cuttlefish must avoid being seen if it is to survive for long. Fortunately for them, nature has equipped cuttlefish, and its other cephalopod relatives, such as octopus and squid, with a mesmerising defence: ultra-fast colour change.

Being highly mobile, cuttlefish swim across the sea floor and into many different habitats, changing colour in real time as they do so; in fact, in less than a second, an individual can go from a pale sandy-yellow texture to presenting strong dark contrasting markings that blend in perfectly with pebbles and rocks. The

Bioluminescence produced on the underside of the velvet belly lanternshark blends in with light from the surface.

chromatophores in their skin, which contain a range of pigment types, are surrounded by muscles that are under the control of the nervous system and linked to the eyes. When the animal sees a new background, it morphs in an instant to match it. Other cells, such as leucophores and iridophores, act like mirrors underneath the chromatophores, helping the cuttlefish to recreate whites and blues.

To adopt such rapid and accurate changes, one might reasonably assume that the cuttlefish has excellent colour vision. Surprisingly, though, they are colour blind and unable to tell apart any of the colours in the ocean, at least, not with their eyes. They can perceive variation in brightness, but not hues. So, how can they achieve such impressive matches? One possibility is that they detect differences in how bright or dark the environment is and change colour appropriately. Pale, fine-textured sand tends to be yellow, while dark rocks are often brown, and bright seaweed may be green. Knowing how bright those objects are could serve as a rule

Common cuttlefish, widespread around Europe, make tasty meals for many predators and rely on camouflage day and night to escape.

of thumb for colour too. There is a more tantalising possibility, however. Recently, scientists discovered that opsins exist in the skin of cuttlefish. These are the same visual pigment proteins that are found in the eyes of many animals with colour vision. The science is still in its infancy, but, somehow, it may be that cuttlefish can see colour, or at least detect different wavelengths of light with their skin.

Cuttlefish, and even more so octopus, have another remarkable skill. They can use special groups of muscles to change the texture of their skin, manipulating sections to flatten it or to create bumps and ridges. When faced with a rock covered with seaweed, an octopus not only holds its arms vertically to match it, but also changes its texture to resemble the three-dimensional form of the algae.

The changes can be even more spectacular. The small (less than 10 centimetres long) octopus *Japetella heathi* lives at a range of ocean depths, from a few hundred metres to a thousand metres. Strangely, when individuals are closer to the surface, they use their chromatophore cells to rapidly pull in their tissue pigment and make their bodies transparent; yet, when in deeper water, they spread out pigment to make their bodies red-black in colour. The creatures can rapidly shift between these two forms, as required. The question is, why?

Animals closer to the surface are at risk of being seen as a silhouette from below. Beyond counter-illumination, an effective solution to combat this is to become see-through: if most of the ambient light passes through the animal's body, then there is little of it to see. By contrast, a darker pigmented creature would be easy to spot against the bright sky; but transparency has weaknesses. Although aquatic environments are more conducive to this approach than on land, there is often a slight mismatch in the transmission of light through body tissue and the wider water environment, and, more seriously, light can be scattered inside the animal, bouncing back from whence it came. In shallower, brighter water, this is less of an issue, but when faced with a predator that hunts with bioluminescent searchlights, it's a serious risk. Many deep-sea predators are equipped with special organs from which they shine beams of blue-green or red light to illuminate other animals. As the light from the torch scatters inside a transparent animal, it would appear brighter than the water around it and easy to detect. However, a dark red or black animal, as many deep-sea creatures are, reflects barely any light at all and merges with the gloom around it much better. So the octopus fine tunes its camouflage to more closely match the environment and defeats the search behaviour of its enemies.

Octopuses escape danger by blending into the environment or mimicking other objects. Here, a long-arm octopus hides in the Philippines.

* * *

As amazing as the cuttlefishes' and octopuses' skills are at matching specific objects in the habitat, there exist other creatures that surpass them. Among the most sophisticated are insects in the family Phylliidae, sometimes referred to as 'walking leaves'. These creatures adopt body shapes that are scarcely believable as animals. The match to a real leaf for colour and shape, right down to the presence of apparent leaf veins, is remarkable. Some species adopt the look of a dead leaf, partly in a state of decay, even marked with blotches of mould, or present sections of the body that appear to have been nibbled by a caterpillar or other herbivore. It's difficult to imagine any predator would find these, except by pure luck. Many stick insects more broadly take on the colour, shape and size of twigs,

Rainforests, like those of Borneo, house animals with some of the most remarkable adaptations for survival, not least the camouflage of leaf insects.

sticks and blades of grass. Some even hold their forelegs out in front of them to increase their length and the perception of a dead twig.

Caterpillars also excel in this area. The larvae of the peppered moth are the spitting image of dead twigs: dull, knobbly and often holding a slight bent body posture. Like the cuttlefish, these caterpillars change colour, albeit slowly over days and weeks, to better resemble the branches they live on, transforming from pale green to dark brown. The comparison with cephalopods does not end there, because the caterpillars can make these changes even when their eyes are blindfolded. In the skin of their bodies, the genes that control opsins – which normally underpin colour vision in cells in the eyes – are highly active, suggesting that the larvae can see light and colours with their bodies, independently of their eyes. This sort of discovery, even just a few years ago, would have been thought of more as science fiction than fact, but the potential ability to see different light spectra through the skin has also been discovered in fish and chameleons.

* * *

In the rainforests of Borneo, a *Draco* lizard springs from the trunk of a giant tree and across to another. Like a number of other animals in this region, including the famous 'flying' frogs, the reptiles glide from tree to tree, using extendable skin flaps, supported by elongated ribs. The jungle environment is a vibrant mixture of sights, contrasts and sounds, but if there is one thing that is likely to attract attention, it is movement; indeed, motion has long been known to be the arch enemy of successful camouflage. An animal may be beautifully matched against the background, almost impossible to detect, but the

A moss-mimic stick insect from Costa Rica takes its camouflage to another level.

Peppered moth caterpillars in the UK change colour to match the twigs where they live.

moment it begins to move, attention is drawn to it immediately. The lizards are well concealed against the trees and foliage where they live, but gliding is a dangerous way to get around; not least, as it leaves the reptiles vulnerable to much faster and more agile birds of prey.

As the lizard leaps across the gap, it opens the flaps of skin along its body and glides slowly downwards. In doing so, it reveals the flight membranes to be bright yellow, which bears a close resemblance to the colour of falling leaves from the local trees in the area. The lizard, it seems, does not only rely on looking like the background environment, but goes so far as to masquerade as a leaf spiralling down from the canopy above. There are over 40 species of *Draco* lizards, and lizards from populations that inhabit different regions and forest types have different hues to their flaps, ranging from red to green. The camouflage matches the predominant colours of the leaves that vary in colour with location. Lizards from coastal mangroves have red membranes, to match the red falling leaves, whereas those from lowland forests have membranes that resemble the yellow leaves found there. The membranes even match the size and shape of the local foliage. These creatures are, therefore, superbly adapted to look like the falling leaves in their own area – after all, it would be little use pretending to be a yellow leaf if all those around were red.

* * *

Some environments are particularly challenging and drive animals to come up with ingenious, and diverse, solutions to stay hidden. The rock or tidal pools that occur around much of the world's shores are one such type of habitat. These places are pounded by crashing waves and currents; covered with water at

Movement is risky as it can attract unwanted attention.
Draco lizards take on the appearance of falling leaves to stay safe.

high tide, yet exposed at low tide. They are miniature worlds of contrast. When the tide comes in, cool ocean water bathes the pools and the creatures living there, submerging most of them entirely. The deeper water brings in larger marine predators, including bigger fish and even marine mammals, such as seals. When the tide is out, much of the rocky world is then exposed to air and wind, influxes of freshwater from rain and streams, and the water in the pools can heat up considerably, with evaporation also raising the salinity. Other predators, notably birds, such as gulls, oystercatchers and turnstones, now pose a risk. The animals that live in rock pools need to be made of strong stuff, able to withstand wild extremes and must protect themselves from many different enemies.

Among the creatures at risk are the small fish that dart in and out of the rocks and weed. Shannies, blennies and gobies all reach sizes that would make a good-sized, yet easily manageable meal for a variety of seabirds and even larger predatory fish. Shannies

Life in the intertidal zone is harsh. Shannies and other fish can change colour to blend in with the varied habitat.

are common in the rock pools, often sticking to the same area, yet they must remain hidden against a diversity of backgrounds. Their general coloration is of a well-camouflaged mottled pattern, with blacks, yellows and browns to match both rocks and sand; yet they have another trick to make full use of this – they can rapidly alter their appearance. In about one minute, individuals can become much darker or lighter, helping them to blend in as they swim around and find new places to hide.

Changing colour and pattern for concealment is rather common in nature, but unlike some fish and cephalopods, many creatures do not change so quickly. Another rock-pool creature can dramatically alter its colour, but it takes time. At the lower margins of the rock pools, in the zone where deeper water begins, lives the aptly named chameleon prawn. This small animal is often overlooked by people, not so much due to its diminutive size, but owing to its incredible camouflage. Taken out of context, the prawns are the epitome of colourfulness –

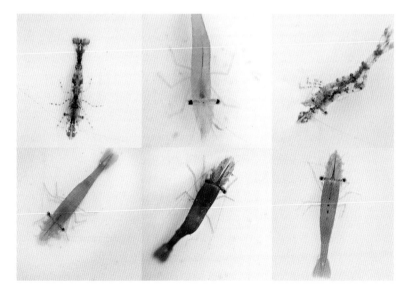

All belonging to one species, these chameleon prawns are common around some UK shores, but easy to miss as they blend in closely with different seaweeds.

they come in different forms, with some a deep purple-red, and others a bright lime-green. A third type is transparent, but marked with intricate patterning; yet they are all a single species. The green individuals match exquisitely green seaweed, such as sea lettuce, whereas others blend in perfectly with red weed, including dulse. The prawns change between these forms, with reds becoming green, and vice versa, but the transformation takes them several weeks. This might seem odd, because, if a prawn is pushed away from its favoured weed to one of a new colour, it will take far too long to take on the hue of its new background. This begs the question of why they bother changing at all. The answer probably comes down to seasonal changes in the algae on which the prawns live. Early in the year the shoreline is dominated with red weed, and, sure enough, the prawns are mainly of the red type. As the season rolls on, the red declines and more brown, yellow and green weed springs up, and the prawns change to better match their new surroundings.

The prawns' strategy of slow change helps them to cope with gradual changes in their habitat, but, as waves and tide knock them from one patch of algae to another, it does not solve the problem of how to keep well hidden in the short term. The prawns even have a solution for this: present red or green prawns with a choice of red or green seaweed, and the individuals will swim to the algae that best matches their own colour.

The existence of the transparent prawns is more of a mystery, yet studies of a closely related prawn, unofficially dubbed the 'carnival prawn' since it lives along the coasts of Brazil, provide the likely answer. The transparent individuals of this species have a streamlined body and are more active swimmers, flitting from one patch of weed to another; in fact, they are mostly males looking for females. For them, there's little value in matching one background closely, so instead they opt for a different approach. They make their bodies transparent, so they are hard to see regardless of the environment in which they are found.

* * *

The diversity of life that exists in the rock pools is also partly a result of the rich variety of miniature habitats that each pool provides. The animals that live here can hide under rocks and in cracks, dart into seaweeds of various colours, or bury themselves in the gravelly seabed. Some use the diverse environment to their advantage, to hide in plain sight, even brazenly wandering around in the open.

Peering into a pool, a small seaweed-covered rock begins to move, slowly making its way from one side of the pool to the other; but this is no rock – it's a long-legged spider crab, a delicate creature with a small triangular-shaped body and spindly

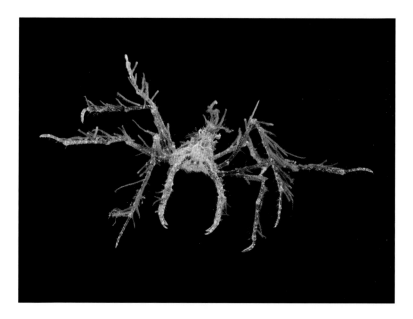

Concealment can be achieved by literally becoming part of the environment, as with the decorations worn by long-legged spider crabs.

legs. This appearance, though, is rarely the one it presents; instead, the body of this spider crab is covered in small hook-like structures onto which it carefully attaches pieces of seaweed. This decorating behaviour means that the crab can wander around in the open and is likely to be mistaken for part of the scenery. The crabs are also in tune with where they live. They modify their seaweed costumes to best resemble the prevailing type that surrounds them, and replace any weed that is no longer sufficiently fresh.

Further away from the shore, in slightly deeper water lives a bigger species, the common spider crab. This beast of the ocean floor has a shell that is more than 20 centimetres across, with long spindly legs and chunky pincers that extend well beyond its considerable torso. It's hard to imagine these mighty crabs having many natural predators, yet clearly they must, for they are often adorned with a range of seaweeds, making them appear not so much like a moving stone but more of a lumbering boulder.

Crabs are protected, to some extent, by a hard shell, and the bigger crabs have thicker exoskeletons, not to mention a pair of intimidating claws to fend off threats. Yet the more diminutive species lack such defences, especially the hermit crabs, which can be barely a few centimetres long. Rather than decorating their bodies with a disguise, they choose objects that provide more robust protection.

The common hermit crab, as its name suggests, is widespread and abundant around UK shores. It is a familiar seashore find, though locating them requires infinite patience, waiting for them to give away their presence when they start to move around. Any small shell, such as that of a whelk, that begins to move a little too fast, may be under the control of a hermit crab. The crab slips its elongated body into the shell, so that only its head and claws emerge, and those it can retract into safety,

A common spider crab from Canada is protected both by its large size and the sponges and seaweed it adds to its body.

Common hermit crabs use shells as safe houses, picking those that match the environment. This shell is also home to small hydroids.

should they need to. As the crabs grow, they must locate larger shells to accommodate their bodies, and this can create fierce competition among them for the choice real estate. There is, however, another requirement for a suitable home, and that is how well it matches the background. Somehow, the hermit crabs are aware of the appearance of the shell they currently occupy, and should a crab find itself living in a light shell but in a dark environment, it will try its upmost to locate a shell of a more suitable colour. The crab's home affords it both physical protection and concealment from threats.

*** *** ***

Coping with the dangers in a single habitat is challenge enough, but some creatures must also remain hidden in the variety of habitats they visit, and even cope with changes as they age. The common or green shore crab is the most widespread and frequently encountered of all UK crabs. Its tolerance of a large range of salinities and temperature and a highly adaptable nature in general mean that it can live in many different habitats; in fact, the crabs have been transported around the world in the ballast of ships and are now one of the most invasive species on the planet. The reference to green, however, is only partially accurate, since while many adult crabs have a dark green hue, there are as many exceptions as crabs that fit the description. Some individuals are pure white, others red-brown or even orange, and often marked with intricate patterns. Juvenile shore crabs are even more diverse, creating a spectacular assortment of colours and contrasts.

One of the most obvious reasons for this colour variation comes from the habitat in which a crab lives. Those inhabiting tidal flats and estuaries take on a brown-green appearance,

*Supremely adaptable, the common shore crab uses colour change
and camouflage to blend in with numerous habitats.*

perfect to blend in with the muddy brown sediment and layers of green algae. Those living in rock pools and mussel beds tend to be much more clearly marked with patterns and have a range of colours on their shells, perfect for those more visually complex environments. This has little to do with genetic differences, for crabs from the same population, living in adjacent habitats, will differ in colour. In the short term, young shore crabs can vary in how bright or dark they are, shifting their appearance one way or the other over a period of a few hours. This helps them to fine tune their appearance and blend into the background, but it does not greatly enhance their camouflage. Instead, much like the chameleon prawns, over a period of weeks, especially as the crabs moult and replace their exoskeletons, they substantially alter their looks to take on the characteristics of their immediate environment – although it's not quite as simple as that.

Crabs from mudflats are excellent at adopting the appearance of that environment. This is in no small part owing to the fact that mudflats are relatively simple habitats visually, so it is easy to adopt an appearance, often one that is relatively devoid of strong patterns, which blends in effectively. By contrast, rock pools are extremely diverse, with reds, greens, yellows, white and black, and other colours originating from the diversity of rocks, gravel and seaweed found there. Taking on the coloration of this environment, let alone the pattern, is far from easy. Were a crab to become red, for example, it would stand out against the green or yellow seaweed and sandy rock-pool bottom. This poses a big problem, since the crabs move about a great deal while foraging. Crabs in rock pools seem not to try and match the habitat at all, but instead, develop markings and colours that are highly variable and of high contrast – blacks and whites, with prevalent shapes such as diamonds, Y-shapes and more besides. They utilise disruptive camouflage to break up their outline, destroy the appearance of shape and blend into the environment more effectively. In the mudflats, there would be no point in adopting disruptive markings; in fact it could be costly, since the high contrast of the patterns would stand out against the relatively featureless environment. Shore crabs, however, rather like the prawns, have another trick up their sleeve. They can choose to reside in areas and background types that are most similar to their coloration, making the most of their individual appearance.

There is another curious feature of shore crab colour, and one that explains why one of their common names is the 'green shore crab'. Crabs change appearance as they grow older and larger, a feature found in many species and usually involves well-camouflaged juveniles becoming more uniform and losing their striking markings as they grow up. Many adult shore crabs take on a green coloration as they grow larger, and there are several reasons why. Older, bigger crabs are less at risk from predators than the juveniles, and so they may not need such good camouflage. This may be partly true, but there's more. The adult crabs tend to move around a lot, often travelling longer distances away from the nursery sites where they grew up, which takes them across a range of habitats and backgrounds. There's little point in trying to match each habitat because it would soon be ineffective as the crab moved on; instead, the crabs seem to use a jack-of-all-trades coloration, which does not resemble the features of any environment perfectly, but one that is a very good match right across the board.

BEHIND THE SCIENCE

A guidebook to insects will quickly reveal that many well-camouflaged moths come in several distinct colour forms, or morphs. In fact, beyond moths, an assortment of other animals also rely on concealing colours, and they too exist in different colour types. There are many reasons for this. A variety of lizards from the United States, for example the eastern fence lizard and little striped whiptail from New Mexico, have camouflage patterns that resemble the places where they live, typically being darker on volcanic rocks and lighter in sandy locations. Unlike the shore crabs, which can change appearances, the lizards form separate populations, and genetic differences underlie their colour types. Over time, predators in each habitat have picked off the lizards that are less well hidden, driving each population to better blend in with the local environment.

Sometimes, the predominant colour forms and their relative frequency change over time. The most widely known example of this evolution in action is the peppered moth. Prior to the Industrial Revolution in Britain, the moth occurred as a pale colour variety, well matched to lichens growing on the branches and trunks of trees in deciduous woodland. When industrial processes took off, however, pollution killed off the lichens and darkened the tree bark with soot. By chance, a new moth form arose, stemming from a mutation to one of the genes that control moth colour, which was darker in appearance and much better matched to the blackened trees. The dark form, therefore, was well concealed from the eyes of hungry birds and more likely to survive, while the pale moths were picked off. As a result, the species shifted dramatically in just a few decades to be dominated by dark moths. With the passing of the Clean Air Acts of the 1950s and 1960s, pollution declined and lichens slowly recovered in some regions of the UK. What followed was that the pale morphs were then better hidden again, while the dark morph stood out, and today the peppered moth exists mostly in its pale form.

The existence of different morphs is not necessarily due to the need to match different backgrounds, but rather to hinder the way that many predators search for food. In the process of hunting, many animals, such as birds, change how they focus their attention after they have found prey animals of a given type. Should a predator come across such prey, it becomes tuned in to finding more of the same thing. If a bird sees several moths that are pale with black spots, for example, they focus their attention on looking for moths that fit this description. It is called a 'search image'. Humans do much the same thing. If we have an idea in our mind of something we need to buy in a shop, we can more effectively find it in among the clutter of other items. The cost with a search image is that the animal looking can miss other potentially rewarding things; a bird looking for a pale moth might overlook an insect right in front of it that is dark with stripes, even if that insect is no better matched to the background than the pale moth. Such searching behaviour by predators has driven some moths to evolve multiple forms, because it makes it harder for predators to find them. There are important implications too. Specifically, if the population of moths is mostly of pale ones, then predators will form a search image for these, but any other types, such as a dark form, will have a disproportionately higher chance of being overlooked. In time, those moths do well and subsequently increase in frequency and become more common; that is, until they reach the point when the darker moths are abundant, and other rarer types of moth, which now look very different, do better. These processes mean that the frequency of different moth types can fluctuate over time, with different forms increasing or declining in abundance compared to the other morphs.

With shore crabs, the high diversity in juvenile forms, especially in rock pools, may enable those crabs to match different visual backgrounds and to use disruptive markings to break up their outline, but it likely also helps them to exploit predator search images. By coming in many colour patterns, predators find it harder to find them. Shore crabs, on many levels, may seem to be remarkably equipped to cope with the pressures from the environment, but they are far from immune to impacts from the human world. While their adaptability may make them highly invasive species outside of their natural range, research has shown that they can be stressed by features of the modern environment, not least noise from ships. Crabs that are exposed to this sound pollution are less likely to run away from danger and less able to change their camouflage colour, which means they are more likely to be found by predators.

* * *

Colour variation is a feature of many camouflaged animals, but the colour patterns adopted tend to be rather dull, as we would expect. However, some creatures take this approach far more extravagantly than others, displaying markings that would normally be seen on costumes used in mating displays or as warning signals. The coastal region of eastern Cuba is a biodiversity hotspot, with mountains, forests and many different marine habitats. Such diverse ecosystems bring to mind colourful birds or beautifully marked butterflies, yet this area is home to an animal that is perhaps even more vibrant – a snail. Cuba is hardly lacking in snails, with 1,400 species of land snail alone, all coming in a variety of colour forms, but it is the Cuban painted snail that stands out.

The painted snail's scientific name is *Polymita picta*, where picta means 'the tattooed' or 'the painted'. This is an apt description;

Cuban painted snails have been described as the world's most beautiful snail. They show enormous variation in their coloration, and it has been suggested this could help confuse bird predators.

each individual is incredibly colourful in its own right, brushed with bright reds, stunning yellows and other colours, and individuals differ markedly from one another. Many animal species, especially invertebrates, have striking individual colours, but the reasons are often mysterious. Here, as with the more muted colours of many camouflaged creatures, the high variation may hinder predators in their search behaviour. If a hungry bird finds a red snail, it may form a search image and focus its attention on finding other red individuals. As a result, yellow snails may go unnoticed. Given a population of red snails, evolution favours individuals that are yellow, until yellows become common and other colours are favoured instead. Rather like some moths, over time, many varieties arise and spread, to the point that a species may be marked with an almost endless diversity of colour patterns. The excessive adornment of the shells of Cuban snails perhaps enhances the tendency for predators to search for the same colour types; a bright red shell may be so striking that a predator can't help but look for more of the same.

***

In nature, the use of different appearances is often tightly linked to the behaviour of the animal possessing it. As with the chameleon prawns in rock pools, this includes where creatures decide to come to rest. Back in the 1950s, scientists were beginning to show that some moths could choose to alight on different-coloured backgrounds, and that they tended to choose backgrounds that matched their own appearance. This is true across different species of moth, with darker species preferring darker backgrounds, but is also the case in moths that come in distinct morphs. The peppered moth, in its pale and dark form,

The Indian leaf-mimic butterfly favours alighting on dead twigs and branches where its camouflage works best.

conforms to this, whereby pale moths prefer to rest on light backgrounds and dark moths on dark backgrounds. As dawn draws near and the moths must begin searching out places to hide on trees, they select places to reside that match their coloration. Selecting the right place to land is critical, since camouflage patterns only work when tied to the backgrounds that they have evolved to resemble.

Some moths take this approach to a more refined level. In South Korea, the moth *Jankowskia fuscaria* is wonderfully well matched to tree bark. When individuals align with the tree trunks they don't simply sit still. Instead, individuals shuffle about until their body position blends in most effectively with the contrasts and crevices of the bark. Individuals only do this if they need to – if, by chance, their initial landing position is a good one, then they stay put.

The eggs of Japanese quail are beautifully marked, with shades of white, yellow or brown, and overlaid with a delicate range of spots and stipples. These are ground-nesting birds. They don't build a structured nest in a tree or other vegetation, but lay their eggs on a patch on the ground. The eggs laid by different females do not come in distinct morphs, but instead, may be a little bit darker than others, or have more pronounced or larger markings; so, across the species, there is a broad spectrum of forms, with each female laying one consistent type.

The precise location that quail choose to nest is important, not least, if a bird with sandy-yellow eggs mistakenly opts to nest on a dark brown background. A mother quail will avoid this, if she has eggs that are light and speckled. She will tend to select backgrounds on which to nest that match the colour of her eggs. In the same way, a bird laying dark eggs with strong large patterns will choose the relevant background. By doing so, the birds can ensure that their own eggs are best matched to local conditions and so are less likely to be seen by birds of prey and egg-eating mammals.

The variety in colour patterns on Japanese quail eggs helps conceal them from predators.

BEHIND THE SCIENCE

Camouflage patterns cannot work on their own. An animal's behaviour is critical for that camouflage to work. Any green creature that chooses to sit on a yellow background would stand out like a sore thumb. Concealing costumes are only effective against the background they are intended to match, and many creatures adopt a range of behaviours that optimise the effectiveness of their disguise. Aegean wall lizards in Greece will choose to sit on rocks that match their individually unique coloration, much like the nesting quail and moths. In other cases, different behaviours are needed to complete the disguise. A variety of caterpillars hold their body in a bent posture, such that the resemblance to a branch is more complete. Stick insects are well known to move their body in sync with the vegetation. Movement can give an animal away, but so too can staying still at the wrong time. If the background vegetation is being blown by the wind, holding a rigid position will only serve to reveal the insect. So, stick insects sway their body forwards and backwards, matching the movement of their bush or tree.

A key question is how animals can actually make the right decisions. How does a moth or a bird, for example, know what its specific colour is and therefore where to sit? In many cases, scientists don't know for sure, but there are several options. One is that the animal can literally use vision to compare its own coloration to that of the surroundings. This might sound challenging, but the placement of the eyes of many creatures and the wide-angle view they afford mean that the bearer could see parts of its own body and that of the background and then compare how closely they match. Some grasshoppers do this and when their body is painted with a different colour, they choose to sit on different backgrounds that match their new form. This approach seems not to be so common in moths. Instead, there seems to be a link between genes that control individual appearance and behaviour. Genes that make a moth a pale colour will also be linked to genes that make the animal prefer light substrates.

Another mechanism seems to enable birds to nest in the right place. Many birds that lay camouflaged eggs produce several broods over the season and in the years that follow. At first, they may, as new mothers, be naïve about what their eggs look like, but, once they have produced a few clutches, they will have learnt and will modify their nesting behaviour accordingly. As the chicks hatch, they might also imprint on the environment where they grow up, so that when they come to breed, often with similar eggs to their own mother, they also choose the same backgrounds. Certainly, some birds such as quail are capable of learning to recognise what their own eggs look like, so while these ideas are somewhat unproven, they are likely to be at least part of the answer.

In the burnt fields and Miombo woodland of the Zambian dry season, a host of ground-nesting birds are breeding. The intense heat is a major threat to the embryo developing in each egg, but so too are nest predators. Baboons and vervet monkeys are always on the lookout for unguarded nests. The eggs are protein-rich fast food, not to mention the odd adult bird that gets careless and is grabbed. Bush shrikes and other avian threats use their keen eyesight to spot nests, and watching them are mongooses, which are cued in to the nest nearby.

With so many opportunists crowding into the area, camouflage is critical to the survival of both the nesting adults and their young, but not all use it in the same way. As danger approaches, a mother three-banded plover flees the nest. She does this while there is still sufficient distance, 10 metres or more, between her and the danger, hoping that she can slink off without attracting attention to the whereabouts of the nest. Should a predator continue to approach, she might try to distract it by feigning injury, or just visibly trying to attract attention to her and not the nest area. Not far away, a Mozambique nightjar sits absolutely still on her nest, enduring the intense heat bearing down on the open field. Even as danger gets close, less than a metre away even, she doesn't move.

The two strategies of the plover and nightjar are reflected across many of their kind. Nightjars tend to sit tightly on their eggs until almost trodden on. In fact, they can certainly make an unsuspecting hiker jump when bursting for cover as a boot comes just a little too close. The reason is that the adult nightjars are adorned with incredible camouflage. Mozambique nightjars blend in with the dark, burnt earth where they nest, whereas, close by,

A camouflaged Mozambique nightjar keeps an eye out for danger.

fiery-necked nightjars have patterns that merge with the leaf litter and break up their outlines under patches of woodland. Most impressive are freckled nightjars, whose plumage seems to be an almost unbroken extension of a large granite rock. The survival of adult nightjars and their clutches relies on their camouflage, and so their eggs are not well hidden. After all, the eggs are rarely exposed, so they have little to gain from camouflage patterns. Should a predator get close enough that an adult must flee, then it's probably game over in any case. Plovers, on the other hand, flee from the nest early, hoping that they can escape before a predator knows a nest is nearby. The adults are not well matched to the environment, but their eggs are. Given that the eggs are often left in the open, exposed to a predator close by, they need to blend in well, or else they will be seen.

The behaviour of the adult plover and nightjar is in tune with the camouflage of their eggs and themselves. This is further reflected in their choice of nest site. Adult plovers choose to nest in locations that provide the best camouflage for their own eggs. By contrast, nightjars choose suitable nest sites that allow the adults to be most effectively hidden. Much like the Japanese quail, the birds and their eggs show a continuum of variation within each species: some individuals and their eggs are darker or lighter, and others are more or less speckled. The choices the adults make reflect their own unique individual colours, or those of their own egg types.

The missing link between the eggs and adult birds is, of course, the chicks. As they grow, the chicks become increasingly mobile, wandering further and further from the original nest site, so they are also well camouflaged, matching the habitat in which their species nests. They crouch down and remain still at the first sign of danger, and some species go even further.

Another bird found in the same Zambian habitats and elsewhere in sub-Saharan Africa is the bronze-winged courser. The chicks of this bird live in relatively open fields, often recently burnt with tufts of charred grass and dark earth, and so the young, appropriately, look almost exactly like of a tuft of singed grass: light yellow feathers close to the body, with spiky dark brown-black tufts sticking further out. It's a remarkable case of a vertebrate that seemingly tries to mimic an object in the environment.

* * *

Across the barren, lichen-covered rocks and tundra of Iceland, a gyrfalcon is hunting. Its keen eyesight and agile movements make it a deadly predator, and it favours one meal in particular: ptarmigan. This medium-sized member of the grouse family accounts for over four-fifths of the falcon's diet, and a large proportion of ptarmigan, especially males, do not make it through an entire year. Being under such a constant risk of attack means that the ptarmigan must have some very effective ways to avoid being eaten.

As with many animals, ptarmigan change colour from summer to winter: white in the winter to match snow, and brown in the summer to blend in with the rocks and low-lying vegetation. Unlike creatures such as crabs and cuttlefish, the changes the birds make are not triggered by what the animal sees, but by changes in day length. A shortening of the daylight hours signifies that winter is on the way, and soon it will be time to moult to white plumage.

Changing colour is no doubt an effective way to match strongly seasonal environments, but the male birds do something odd: they delay their colour change in spring by several weeks, and in the process their white costume is highly visible in the snowless landscape. By standing out, they appear more attractive to females and more likely to mate. The cost, of course, is the heightened risk of being eaten and, once a male has mated, it still takes him several

Overleaf: Surviving the harsh winter in Svalbard, Norway, ptarmigan adopt their winter plumage to blend in with the snow.

weeks to make the transformation – that's a long time to survive with such a poorly matched plumage. By bathing in soil and mud, though, male ptarmigan can combat this risk, making their feathers dark to match the ground, an effective way to hide while waiting for their new set of feathers to grow. Ptarmigan also appear to behave in a manner that is well suited to their current costume. Female birds that have changed to a flecked brown coloration will shun patches of snow and scurry off when they mistakenly wander across them. Males with mismatched costumes will also try to hide under rocks and other shelters.

These birds are not the only animals to change colour with the season. In North America snowshoe hares switch between brown and white coats, and they too are under intense risk of predation, not just from birds of prey, but also coyotes, wolves and bobcats. Unfortunately for the hares, climate change is reducing the duration of snow cover in many regions and making it less predictable, meaning that hares are increasingly likely to be mismatched with their environment and get eaten as a result. Unlike the ptarmigan, they show much less awareness of their background and current coloration, failing to sit on the most appropriate backgrounds, even when there is a choice of snow and bare ground. Hare numbers may suffer heavily as climate change becomes more severe.

Another mammal with a white pelage, and which also uses it for camouflage, is a remarkable little bat – the Honduran white bat, which lives in the jungles of Latin America. The way its defence system works is rather unusual. White fur might seem foolish in a green forest, but mammals cannot grow green fur – the closest they get is the green fur of sloths, which is due to the growth of green algae. The bats remedy this by roosting in small groups at night, when they construct little tents. By gently cutting out and pulling leaves together, they build a shelter to hide in during the day. Inside, the roost is bathed in green light, which reflects off the bats' bodies, making them appear green. It's an ingenious way to hide even with completely mismatched fur, by using a trick of the light.

* * *

Sometimes, camouflage can be rather counter-intuitive, to the extent that colours, which to us appear almost dazzling, can afford concealment in nature. As well as Honduran bats, there is a selection of bugs and beetles that exists in striking blues and greens, their bodies shimmering in the sunlight. The specific hue that they take on is changeable; their iridescent colours coming from structural mechanisms, in which light interacts with multiple layers of body cuticle, spaced in a variety of arrangements. Among the most extravagant are the jewel beetles – a large group of over 15,000 species, many of which appear as glimmering metallic bodies, changing with the light and with the angle from which they are seen. It may seem hard to imagine that the appearance of these creatures is for concealment, but they are usually seen out of context, in museum collections. Under natural conditions, they blend in rather than stand out.

The suggestion that jewel beetles and other iridescent insects may use their coloration for camouflage comes from the fact that many are largely green in colour, albeit a bright shiny green, but which can take on blue, purple and other iridescent hues. The question that puzzled scientists, however, was whether the iridescence itself could afford protection from predators. It seems it can. Beetles that have true iridescent markings are less likely to be seen by birds than beetles that are a range of matt colours, or even those that are just shiny green. Quite why iridescence works is less clear, but it may function by fooling what the brain is looking for. The eye of an animal might be drawn to a bright shiny object of

one colour, say a metallic blue, but as the predator moves closer the insect's colour changes, perhaps to green, and the predator can't find the blue object it was searching for.

Something very similar was suggested by Victorian naturalists to explain iridescence in butterflies, including the shiny bright morpho butterflies from South America. Their dazzling colours sparkle and interact with shafts of sunlight in the forest, before disappearing or changing as the butterfly moves. Scientists have also shown that birds find it hard to track small moving objects that have iridescent colours. For some reason, the changing hues confuse their tracking skills, and, when they strike, they often miss the target.

* * *

There is one enigmatic animal, whose colour has remained mysterious for hundreds of years, with scores of theories to explain its appearance, many centred on camouflage, and that's the zebra. These members of the horse family are found in large herds on the open African savannah, where they make a good meal for predators, such as lions and hyenas.

Some of the theories to explain the striking black and white stripes of zebra focus on how the stripes may be used in mating, or for recognising individuals; after all, each zebra has its own pattern They might even be a good warning sign to predators that the zebra are strong and have a powerful kick, something any chasing lion should be careful to avoid. None of these ideas, though, has had much if any support. Another suggestion is that the black and white stripes set up air currents over the animal's body, serving to cool it down in the intense heat. This has gathered some backing, but it seems unlikely to be the main driver for the zebra's unusual costume.

The mysterious function of the stripes has time and time again been suggested to play a role in camouflaging the animals,

The shiny iridescent colours of a rainbow jewel beetle from Brazil may help it blend in.

Bright sparkling dorsal wings on a blue morpho in flight could confuse predator attacks.

perhaps against trees or woodland. At first, this does not seem a very sensible idea – anyone who has seen zebra in the open knows how visible they are, and they are not a mainly woodland species, but things are not so simple. Lions do not see colours as well as we do and often hunt at twilight. Perhaps, the zebra stripes merge into the environment at dusk, with some of the markings breaking up the outline in a disruptive manner. Alas, there is little to support this idea either. A further suggestion is that the black and white stripes may interfere with how a predator sees movement, a little like iridescence, and dazzle the attacker into misjudging both the direction and speed of a fleeing animal, so the predator mistimes its attack. This may be especially apt when trying to track a single zebra in a herd, with a confusion of black and white stripes moving about all over the place. Dazzle has some support in other circumstances and may be a plausible reason for the markings on some snakes, so it's not out of the question here. However, for obvious reasons, this is a rather tricky idea to test in practice with lions and zebra.

Lions watching a zebra herd in the Maasai Mara National Reserve, Kenya – but do the zebra stripes really deter predators?

The science of zebra coloration had been rather stuck, until biologists began to consider more seriously another major threat to them: biting insects, such as the tsetse fly. These large blood-sucking insects are not just a nuisance, but transmit a variety of dangerous diseases and are a major threat to a zebra's health. For some reason, zebra have thinner skin than other horses, making them more susceptible to the flies. This may be where the answer lies. Tsetse and other biting flies tend to avoid landing on stripy black and white objects. It's not clear why, but it may be that, as the insects approach the zebra, their visual system is fooled by the relative movement of the stripes, meaning that the flies either avoid landing or simply cannot approach the target accurately. While the mysterious nature of the zebra stripes is not entirely solved, it seems that it more likely comes down less to escaping flies than to avoiding lions.

✳ ✳ ✳

We tend to think of camouflage as the dominion of animals, but this is not entirely true. High up, on the mountain slopes of Yunnan province, China, the environment is unforgiving. It is, for one thing, very open and exposed, and the mountainsides are often composed of steep scree slopes, characterised by rocks of varying colours. In some areas, the rocks are mostly light grey, whereas elsewhere they may be darker, or red-brown. In these habitats lives a variety of unusual plants, including *Corydalis hemidicentra*, whose leaves are exceptionally well camouflaged. The leaves of this species have an elongated oval shape, with colours ranging from deep red-brown to pale grey, each type tightly matching the local rock colour and even the shapes of the rocks. Local plant populations, separated by the steep mountain slopes, have evolved on virtual islands, each population with its own characteristic camouflage colours. The camouflage works against herbivores, not least to hide from Apollo butterflies that wish to lay their eggs on the plants, which become food for their caterpillars. Butterflies often have good colour vision, and a green host plant against a grey or red rocky slope would stand out like a beacon, not least with little other vegetation to hide in on the harsh mountain sides. By matching the colour of the rocky environment, they can blend in. The plants also delay producing flowers, to attract bees, until after the butterflies have finished laying eggs. Those plants that live in regions with a greater risk of being used as hosts have evolved better camouflage to combat this.

Having such drastically modified leaf colour may pose a significant cost for plants, since the typical green coloration more usually seen comes from chlorophyll, essential for photosynthesis. It may be for this reason that camouflaged plants are uncommon; or simply that we have not been looking for them until recently. Yet other examples do exist. 'Living stone' plants from South Africa, for example, masquerade as … stones. They also appear in colour forms that seem better matched to the local environment, and likely evolved the deception to avoid being eaten by grazing herbivores. It is not just the plants themselves that adopt camouflage: the seeds of some Californian plants, such as those of Chilean bird's-foot trefoil, match the colour of the local soil. The soil where the plants live often varies between grey and brown, and the colour of the seeds from plants in these localities varies to match the local environment to reduce the chances of being consumed by birds. Far from being only green, and using colours simply in flowers to attract pollinators, scientists are discovering more and more plants that conceal themselves instead and depart from the stereotyped green form.

***

Camouflage enables creatures to go unnoticed in the great range of habitats where they live. The methods used are truly diverse and often ingenious, from the bioluminescent counter-illumination of sharks to the transparent bodies of frogs and octopuses. Appearances are often flexible, able to cope with a variety of backgrounds and seasons, with creatures following the changes in habitat over time, or morphing between forms as they move around. Concealment is also reliant on behaviour, and creatures from birds to moths somehow know where to sit and even at what angle to rest. In some regards, camouflage is the ultimate type of illusion – fooling another animal that you do not exist at all, or being mistaken for something completely different. Yet deception goes far beyond camouflage, and tricksters of all sorts abound in nature.

Stone plants in the Namibian desert might easily be mistaken for inedible rocks by hungry herbivores.

CHAPTER SIX

DECEPTION

In the forests of Malaysia, a bee is circling around a
flower, deciding whether or not to land. The flower, a
bright pinkish-white set against the deep green of
the background foliage, glows like a beacon,
attracting the attention of pollinators far and wide.
But this is no ordinary flower. It is not a plant at all,
but an insect – an orchid mantis. The bee lands, and
this spells its end. The mantis strikes with its
raptorial forelegs and begins to feast.

It's not difficult to see where the orchid mantis gets its name, but its deception is a marvel of nature. Not only does the colour of the insect resemble a flower, but also its entire morphology, right down to the intricate shapes of its legs: they resemble leaf petals, and the colour does not simply match that of real flowers, but is brighter and more vivid than the petals of the real thing. By exaggerating its colour signal, the mantis becomes even more irresistible to pollinating insects, which are lured in close enough for the predator to strike.

The mimicry and exaggerated display of the orchid mantis have evolved to help it obtain more food. Were it not for this, the predator would have to rely on insects coming close enough by chance alone. By resembling a flower, and a super-bright one at that, the mantis can stack the odds more in its favour. It should almost go without saying that, for all creatures, life is a challenge. Finding food, attracting a mate, and avoiding being eaten take time and energy, and reflect a delicate balance between risk and reward. Any way that an animal can get ahead of the game is likely to be favoured in evolution. This can involve cheating the system, sometimes extravagantly. Trickery is commonplace in the natural world, and is used in a wondrous variety of ways, not least in obtaining food, from stealing it from under the noses of others to luring prey to their doom. On the other hand, many animals use deception to stay alive, including conning potential foes that the bearer is not worth attacking at all, or even falsely pretending to be something harmful. And, because ultimately all creatures are driven to reproduce and pass on their genes, cheating is widespread when it comes to securing a mate, and even raising young.

* * *

A Malaysian orchid mantis lures prey to their doom by pretending to be a bright pink flower.

Many of us know first-hand that a sting from a wasp is unpleasant enough to warrant future caution. The wasp's yellow and black banding patterns act as a clear warning signal. The message the colours convey is an honest one: the wasp has a defence worth avoiding. The insect benefits from not being attacked, and the predator (or human) benefits by not being stung. Yet, when truthful communication systems like this exist in nature, they are often ripe for being exploited by others.

In any park or garden there is likely to be an abundance of hoverflies during the summer months. These harmless flies, performing their aerial acrobatics, take several vital roles in the ecosystem, not least as important pollinators. But being undefended means that they are vulnerable to attack, especially from birds. A variety of species therefore adorn themselves with

Not a bumblebee but a convincing mimic: the hoverfly **Volucella bombylans.**

yellows, oranges and blacks, creating the impression of a stinging insect. In some cases, the deception can be marvellously convincing and nuanced. The hoverfly *Volucella bombylans* is a striking copy, or mimic, of bumblebees, but not just any bumblebee. This species of fly comes in two main types: one that bears close resemblance to white-tailed bumblebees, and one that mimics red-tailed bumblebees. The deception is so well developed that the flies even copy the bees' buzzing sounds. If you hold an agitated hoverfly in your hand, the noise can be quite disconcerting.

These, and numerous other creatures, are examples of Batesian mimicry, named after the famous Victorian naturalist-explorer Henry Walter Bates. When travelling in the Amazon rainforest, Bates discovered that many completely harmless butterflies are not attacked by birds because they have the same wing coloration, and even the same ponderous flight behaviour, as butterflies that carry toxins in their bodies. By copying the warning signals of others, the butterflies can afford protection for themselves by creating uncertainty in the minds of predators as to whether or not to attack. Bates's discoveries were published not long after Charles Darwin's *Origin of Species* and provided some of the first clear supporting evidence for natural selection in nature, much to Darwin's delight.

Not all hoverflies resemble bumblebees. The hornet hoverfly, one of the UK's largest and most impressive flies, shows off bright brown-orange and black patterns and, as its common name suggests, closely resembles a hornet. Its considerable size alone is impressive. Not all flies of this group are close mimics, however. For example, whereas the common drone fly is the spitting image of a honeybee, the marmalade hoverfly only loosely copies the yellow and black stripes of a wasp. The existence of these so-called 'imperfect mimics' has long puzzled biologists.

BEHIND THE SCIENCE

In addition to hoverflies, a great variety of insects apparently resemble wasps, hornets and bees for defence. For some, the match is scarcely believable at times: the lunar hornet moth is so close in coloration, body shape and even transparent wings to a wasp or hornet that one often has to look several times to see through the disguise. On the other hand, although the wasp beetle displays the yellow and black markings found on many stinging insects, it does not otherwise excel in its level of deception. Why does such variation in the refinement of these disguises exist?

As with many areas of biology, the occurrence of imperfect mimics probably has several explanations. The simplest is that evolution has simply not had the time to work on the appearance of some animals; to fine tune their form and colour to more closely match that of the animal they are copying. Constraints may also limit how closely an animal can perfect its disguise. For example, perhaps the body shape of the wasp beetle is needed for many other aspects of its biology, and adopting a more wasp-like form would compromise other essential functions, such as movement or even recognising their own kind. In the case of many hoverflies, it is not always clear what specific species of stinging insect they are mimicking; in fact, they may adopt a jack-of-all-trades approach, and so look like a generic bee or wasp, but not match closely any specific species. By doing so, the hoverfly might always have stinging insects around it that it broadly looks like, whereas were it to copy a particular species it might be left undefended were that species to disappear, for whatever reason.

There are other, more nuanced, explanations for why imperfect mimics exist. One of these is that mimicry needs to be better when the animal is a more attractive target for a predator. For example, a big juicy hoverfly is a more rewarding meal than a tiny scrawny one, and sure enough, the degree of mimicry in hoverflies is higher when the insects are larger. Big flies are simply more likely to be attacked, so must invest more in a good defence. Additionally, the risk of attack also depends on how dangerous the animal being copied is. A large aggressive wasp, with a powerful sting, carries a more forceful punch than a timid bee with a mild sting that is reluctant to attack, except as a last resort. So hoverflies and other creatures may get away with less convincing mimicry if the animal they resemble is more dangerous – it's simply not worth a predator trying its luck.

This marmalade hoverfly looks like a wasp or a bee. It mimics the bold black and yellow stripes of those stinging insects. By copying the colours of more dangerous insects, this harmless fly gains protection from predators.

Batesian mimics do not always have striking colours, especially if the animals they are resembling are correspondingly subdued. Yet they can be every bit as impressive in their deception. Ants are among the most numerous organisms on the planet, both as species and individuals. Their incredible variety and modes of life, especially their high levels of social living, make them hugely successful in most parts of the world. They are also prosperous because ants are frequently well defended, with powerful jaws, strong stings, fierce behaviour and sometimes the capability to squirt acid. With a few exceptions, such as anteaters and green woodpeckers, they do not feature on the menu of most predators.

To resemble an ant, therefore, is to afford a great deal of protection, and a large number of jumping spiders do just that. Their body shape is modified into an elongated form, appearing shiny black or yellow and with an ant-like abdomen. They even walk like ants, holding their front pair of legs in front of their head, like a pair of antennae. Across one genus of jumping

By mimicking ants, some jumping spiders, like this one from northeast Madagascar, gain protection from other predatory spiders.

spiders called *Myrmarachne*, which contains probably over 100 species, most if not all of their members mimic ants. The main driving force for this is not to escape vertebrate foes, like birds, but rather other spiders. Jumping spiders are notorious predators, with extremely refined vision, excellent for seeing colour and fine detail. They creep up on their prey and, when close enough, they pounce. In many respects, they are the invertebrate world's tiger equivalent, albeit equipped with better colour vision and a wider angle of view around their body. For many jumping spiders, their favoured food is other spiders, including other jumping spiders. Scientists have shown that, by displaying the colour and shape of ants, those prey spiders, which would normally be attacked, are avoided by their predators – the spiders doing the hunting treat the mimics as if they are ants. Sometimes the mimicry is extraordinary, even occurring at a collective level across entire groups of spiders. The dark-footed ant-spider from Central Africa, for example, lives in groups of 10 to 50 individuals, and collectively they behave like a swarm

An ant-mimicking jumping spider sits on a leaf below a group of green tree ants in Sri Lanka.

of ants. This enables the spiders to obtain food and stay safe, much more so than a lone individual.

The use of colour to mimic other animals for protection tends to be the domain of invertebrates, but there are striking exceptions. In the forests of Peru lives a bird called the cinereous mourner that, as an adult, is rather dull and grey, but its chicks could hardly be more different.

Sitting in the nest, the young have vivid orange feathers, outlined with black and tipped with white. They bear a striking resemblance to locally occurring very hairy and toxic caterpillars. When threatened, the chicks crouch down, swaying their bodies from side to side, just like wriggling caterpillars. Only when a parent comes with food and makes an appropriate call do the young revert to type and look like actual chicks. Nest predation on these birds is very high, and the defence has evolved to counteract this, putting off any predators that would normally be repulsed by large noxious caterpillars.

***

In the gloomy understory of the rainforests of Costa Rica, an eye can be made out on a tree. A dark pupil, with white specs of reflection, is surrounded by a bright yellow iris – the eye of a bird of prey, such as an owl or hawk, surely. Actually, no. This 'eyespot' belongs to an owl butterfly.

In the dim conditions, and set against the dull background of the butterfly's wing colouring, the eyespot bears a convincing resemblance to that of a bird of prey; but why? The answer is for defence. An owl butterfly, which is an impressive size, would make a tasty meal for a range of forest birds and reptiles, so what better way to protect itself than by presenting an impression of its predators' own enemies? In the gloom, a bird might do well

In the gloom of the Costa Rican rainforest, a small bird might mistake the spot on an owl butterfly as a predator's eye staring back.

to be wary of what looks like a bright eye staring back. To stay away from the butterfly, though, might mean a lost meal, but to venture too close to a real predator could result in the loss of its own life. It's worth being cautious.

The eyespot on the owl butterfly is essentially always on display when the insect is at rest. When sitting on a tree trunk or the forest floor, the butterfly's wings stay closed, but with the spot visible. The defence probably works by reducing the chance that a predator would approach the insect in the first place. When at rest, by contrast, an eyed hawk-moth perches in a tree with its forewings beautifully well camouflaged against the branches and trunk, concealing the underwings below. When approached too closely, especially if actually touched by a predator, the moth flashes open its wings to reveal two impressive and colourful spots on its hind wings, accompanied by shimmering erratic movement. This is a startle display. Opinion may vary on how effectively the red and blue of the spots form a convincing mimic of a real eye, but if a predator, such as a robin perhaps, is suddenly faced with two bright circles staring back, they would be best placed to play it safe and fly away.

Eyespots are common in nature, especially in butterflies, moths and fish. The peacock butterfly is another impressive example. Each of its gaudy wings is marked with a bright red, blue, yellow and black spot. When under attack, the butterfly flashes open its wings repeatedly, showing off the spots, which are highly effective in preventing the butterfly from being attacked. Studies have shown that, for half an hour or more, birds will repeatedly fly down to attack the butterflies, but every time fly off when startled, before eventually giving up. In this species, the mimicry to real eyes is not close at all – after all, not many predator eyes are blue and red, nor do they have such gaudy asymmetric arrangements of colours – but the flash of bright conspicuous hues and patterns seems enough to deter any small bird.

Deception is also adopted by butterfly and moth caterpillars. In the rainforests of Central and South America, for example, you can find the caterpillar of a species of hawk moth – *Hemeroplanes triptolemus* – camouflaged among the vegetation. At first, it seems harmless, but when threatened, it rears up, showing off its hind end while, at the same time, altering its body shape, so that it forms a triangle marked with two fake eyes. It may be small, but the resemblance in form and movement to a venomous snake is remarkable. So impressive is this display that the caterpillar is said to sometimes dart towards a threat, as if pretending to strike. Henry Bates once found one of these caterpillars while collecting insects in the Amazon. He brought it back to the village in which he was staying, and then proceeded to alarm those living there by showing them the caterpillar in its defensive mode.

Snake mimicry is seemingly found in a number of caterpillar groups, including certain swallowtail butterfly species. Quite often, the larvae do not simply resemble any old generic snake form, but in fact adopt postures and shapes that more specifically match the appearance of vipers. While the caterpillars are very small compared to most snakes, juvenile snakes can sometimes still pack a punch, and in any case, it's seldom worth the risk to a predator to find out. Better to move on and find other things to eat.

From time to time, eyespots can appear in unusual places. Native to South America, the diminutive Cuyaba dwarf frog looks well camouflaged, and harmless enough as a potential meal. When threatened, however, it inflates its body and reveals a pair of large black 'eyes' surrounded by rings of yellow on its rear end. The message is clearly, 'Don't eat me, I'm a bigger

animal than you think,' and the frog has toxins to back up its display, should a predator ignore the warning and try to taste it.

In birds, when we picture eyespots, we might imagine animals such as the famous peacock and its extravagant tail used as a mating signal. South America's sunbitterns also spread their wings to reveal eyespots, but not rows of gaudy ones; rather, single large orange and black spots, which are startling, nonetheless. While these can be used during courtship, the imposing display is also presented when the nest is threatened, to scare away would-be predators.

* * *

In nature, eyespots don't simply work to scare and intimidate potential predators. They can also divert attacks to less vital places. The margins of the ringlet butterfly's wings are lined with small eyespots, each with the characteristic white spot at its centre, together with a black pupil surrounded by a white or yellow iris. Predators often peck and bite conspicuous features on prey, rather like aiming at specific targets; by placing rows of spots along the wing margins, ringlets and other butterflies can induce predators to attack the outer margins of the wings, rather than their more vital bodies. Deflecting a predator's attack might result in a small piece of the wing going missing, but many butterflies can still fly in this condition. Indeed, it is common to find some rather bedraggled butterflies as the summer goes on, some of which have tell-tale 'V-shaped' gaps in the wings, perhaps from the beak of a bird.

Having rows of spots along the wing margins is one way to divert attacks, but some butterflies go even further, taking their deception to another level. A hairstreak butterfly is sitting on a plant stem, its body facing upwards, antennae out in front. Or so

Eyespots on the spicebush swallowtail caterpillar and ringlet butterfly help the bearers stay alive, by deterring and deflecting predator attacks.

By inflating its body and showing two dark eyespots, a Cuyaba dwarf frog no longer makes an attractive meal.

it seems. In fact, it is quite the opposite. On the hind end of the insect is a pair of small false eyes, and the 'antennae' are actually elongations of the hind wings. The body is facing down, ready to fly off should a predator make a strike at the false head. This is a cunning strategy, since birds often attack the head end of insects, partly to incapacitate them, and partly because, by striking at the front the insect, the prey may still be caught at the back end, if it flies off forwards earlier than expected.

Eyespots are widely found in fish too, and frequently they occur at the hind ends of the animal, so also appear to work in deflecting predator attacks. A predator diverts its strike to the eyespots on the fish but, as the fish swims forward, the predator misses. Juvenile Ambon damselfish from the Indo-Pacific coral reefs make a tasty meal for a range of predators. As a defence, their yellow body bears a black eyespot, bordered by a white ring, on the hind area of their dorsal fin. The eyespot is very similar in appearance to the real eyes of the fish. Interestingly,

The fins of many fish are marked with eyespots, as on this Ambon damselfish from Indonesia.

juvenile Ambon damselfish, which are exposed to predators when they are developing, produce larger eyespots than those fish that live in safer settings. Somehow, the fish can perceive how risky the environment is, and invest in a more substantial defence when they are in greater danger. Most likely, the eyespot works by tricking predators, usually other fish, into thinking the damselfish is facing the other direction, and so miscue their attack as the fish flees. To enhance the illusion, damselfish that grow bigger eyespots develop smaller eyes, furthering the likelihood that the predator will mistake the region of the spot for the head end.

Deflecting attacks is not always achieved through circular eyespots. A curious feature of many lizards is that their tails are often different in colour to the rest of the body. In many cases, while the lizard itself is well camouflaged, the tail appears bright blue or another vivid hue. Rather like eyespots, a likely reason is to divert attacks to a part of the body that is relatively expendable. When grabbed, many lizards can, if needed, shed their tails, allowing the lizard to escape while the predator is distracted by the colourful, and sometimes still wriggling, tail. At its base, deliberate fracture lines enable the tail to break off with minimum damage to the rest of the body. The vivid colours of the tail help to make sure that it is easier to see and better at directing attacks to this part while the lizard flees.

Bright tail colours are commonly found in juveniles, which tend to suffer a higher risk of attacks than adults. Young skinks, for example, have gaudy tails for defence, including the American five-lined skink, a common lizard across the eastern USA and into Canada. It has a metallic blue-green tail, which is striking against the dull background of the broken rocky and partially wooded areas in which it lives, and contrasts strongly with the black body with yellow stripes, although the display is found

only in juveniles. As the lizards grow and mature, the tail becomes more camouflaged in colour. Adults are less likely to be at risk, and losing a tail is costly. In fact, the tail is a valuable place to store fat, with up to 50 per cent of the animal's reserves found there. So, for juveniles, it is a cost worth paying to stay alive, whereas the risk of attack is low enough for adults that they can dispense with the defence.

***

The use of deception is not limited to defence, but is also valuable in attack. Deep down in the dark waters of the Atlantic Ocean, a kilometre below the surface, an anglerfish is waiting for a meal. Its enormous jaws, lined with rows of sharp teeth, are ready to strike at anything that comes close. This predator does not simply wait passively for food to blunder into its patch; as its name suggests, it has a more active approach to fishing.

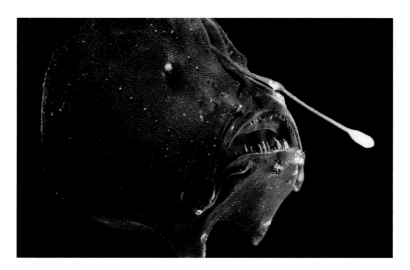

Lured to a detachable blue tail, predators may miss the prize of the body of a five-lined skink from North America.

Searching for prey takes time, so what better way to hunt than to lure food to a glowing fishing rod, as does this deep-sea anglerfish from the Atlantic Ocean?

In the darkness, all that can be seen is a small blue bioluminescent light, glowing and wriggling in the darkness. A small fish is drawn to it – perhaps the light is a potential meal, rare in these ocean depths? The fish gets closer, and then it disappears in a rush of movement, gobbled into the huge jaws of the anglerfish. Under brighter light, the deception is clearer: above the body of the anglerfish, a modified dorsal fin ray extends in front of its head. It's a fishing rod, and at its end is a small organ that houses the symbiotic bacteria that produce the glowing light. It's an effective way to ensure that a meal comes to the anglerfish, without having to search the vast expanses of the deep sea for food. The prey may be drawn to the light out of simple curiosity, inspecting something that grabs its attention and stimulates its visual system strongly. Or it may be entirely fooled into considering the end of the lure as food, before it becomes food itself. Either way, it's the victim of a deadly game of deception.

* * *

Springtime in Australia, and the countryside is brightened by the beauty of flowers of many colours. Sitting on top of a white daisy is a white crab spider, waiting for a meal. To us, the spider and flower are a close match, the spider expertly hidden against the bright petals. Surely, the spider is hiding from its prey so that pollinating insects, like flies and bees, might land on the flower without seeing the threat that exists … But all is not what it seems.

Under ultraviolet light, the spider glows, while the flower is dark, absorbing the UV rays that strike it. This hardly fits the bill for effective concealment, since many pollinators see ultraviolet light perfectly well. It is, however, what the spider intends. Flies and bees tend to be drawn to ultraviolet objects, especially those concerning flowers. UV coloration is common in pollinating

To us, Australia's white crab spider is beautifully camouflaged against a white flower, but scientists now realise there is more to this predator's hunting strategy than hiding. Insect pollinators can see in UV and are attracted to the strong UV markings on the crab spider's body. By glowing in UV, the spider lures more insects to visit the flower.

plants, and many flowers use UV markings, called nectar guides, to direct pollinators to their centre – rather like little landing lights, showing bees where to land. By acting as a UV beacon, the spider exploits this tendency in its flying prey and actively lures the victims directly towards it. Although the spider shape is not much of a match to a real flower, the insects' vision, especially from afar, is sufficiently blurry, and their desire to gather pollen and nectar strong enough, that the disguise works. In fact, bees are more attracted to flowers that have a spider perched on top, than to flowers without one.

This is not the end of the story, however. The spiders do match the flower in other parts of the colour spectrum. Over a period of days they can change colour, from white to yellow, to better match the flower type on which they currently reside, transferring pigments to the outer reaches of their exoskeleton to do so. The spiders are taking a risk by standing out, because they too can end up as dinner, not least for keen-eyed birds. While birds can also see UV, the spider, by matching the flower in other parts of the spectrum, can reduce the risk of being detected by those that it does not intend to attract.

For some reason, similar species of European crab spiders do not use this ultraviolet scam to lure their prey. They genuinely do rely

on camouflage, and closely match the flower throughout the visual range. European pollinators are not, therefore, wise to the Australian spider's tricks, and introduced honeybees readily fall for it. By contrast, native Australian bees are more evasive and have evolved a reluctance to land on flowers with bright UV blobs, even if they are initially drawn to them from afar. They are locked in an evolutionary arms race with the spiders, balancing their attraction to flowers with evolving a resistance to the spider's tricks.

Crab spiders are by no means the only spiders that attract prey with special colours. Many orb web-building spiders do something similar, both with their body coloration and with decorations that they add to their webs.

We might easily assume that spiders' webs are intended to be almost invisible, or at least inconspicuous, so that a variety of flying prey unwittingly crashes into them. But this is often not true. Many spiders add silk structures to their webs that make them much more visible. These decorations often glow strongly in ultraviolet light and are arranged in the shape of a cross or lines running down or diagonally across the web. In the southern UK lives the wasp spider, a beautiful, relatively uncommon creature, with an abdomen marked with yellow and black stripes. Down the centre of its web, it sometimes constructs a zig-zag silk decoration. This may seem foolish if the aim is to hide the web from prey, but it isn't. It's the opposite, and a further clue is that many web-building spiders don't hide, but instead sit in the middle of their web, on full display. Things don't add up if the aim is for the web and spider not to be seen.

As it happens, the UV-reflecting silk structures act rather like the coloration of the Australian crab spiders. Insects are drawn towards them, with a deep instinctive urge to inspect the glowing UV stripe more closely. By doing so, they crash land into the web and their fate is sealed. Many spiders all over the

In the UK, a female wasp spider adorns her web with zig-zag decorations to entice flying insects.

world add web decorations, sometimes large very conspicuous structures that span the whole web. When scientists delicately remove the decorations from the web, or reduce the amount of UV light they reflect, the spiders' webs capture fewer prey items.

But what of the body colour? In the wasp spider, one might assume that its coloration is like that of a hoverfly or wasp beetle, a bluff to deter any would-be predators. This may be true but, in many spiders, it does not seem to be the case. More often, coloration is another device to attract prey, and the bright markings draw them in. Scientists don't know for sure exactly how these markings work, but a good bet is that they lure prey towards them by exploiting a general attraction that prey have to colourful and broadly flower-like objects. When scientists have painted over the spider's markings, or removed spiders from the centre of the web entirely, interception rates of prey decline. So, the very presence of the spider itself helps to increase the amount of food captured. The cost is that, unfortunately for the spider, it can sometimes attract predators too, from wasps to birds. Nature is full of trade-offs.

A European crab spider blends in with the flower on which it sits and waits for prey.

BEHIND THE SCIENCE

Deception is commonplace in the natural world, but it can work in a variety of ways. The first approach is to deceive a watching animal that there is nothing there at all, or that things are not as they seem. For example, the Indian leaf mimic butterfly *Kallima*, from Southeast Asia, pretends to be a dead leaf, hidden in plain sight. Beyond camouflage, disguising oneself as something else entirely is a widespread tactic. To stay alive, many insects pretend to be bees or wasps. Rather than being hidden, a potential predator is duped into considering a hoverfly as an entirely different sort of insect – it sees the fly, but the predator classifies it as something else. In an aggressive context, predators often disguise themselves as harmless creatures, or even other parts of their environment in order to get close enough to their prey to strike, much like the orchid mantis.

Somewhat differently, animals can exploit the ways that sensory systems work, and tap into the stereotyped behaviours that many creatures show. A predator, for example, might present highly visible, colourful patterns or displays that are especially effective at stimulating the visual system of their quarry. In the process, the prey animal is drawn to the vivid colours, much like the way that spiders lure pollinators that are attracted to colourful or ultraviolet markings on flowers. Or, as many cuckoos do, the trickster can present an exaggerated begging display that many host birds can't help but respond to in bringing more food. The key here is not in mimicking something specific, but in exploiting the general way that sensory systems work.

All across the world's coral reefs, fish are visiting cleaner stations, aiming to get some TLC. The fish, called 'clients', are drawn to stations that are set up by cleaner fish, as well as a variety of cleaner prawns and shrimps. The client fish descend to the seabed and indicate that they are ready for a service by turning a dark colour. Then they sit, mouth gaping and gills open, waiting to be attended. This is an important message to convey – the clients are frequently fish of substantial size, which could easily gobble up a cleaner shrimp or fish that was a little too eager. The relationship between cleaner and client is a classic example of mutualism: the client gets nasty parasites, mucus and old skin removed, while the cleaner gets an easy meal. Yet these sorts of situations are ripe for cheats to evolve, and, sure enough, they have.

On the reefs of the Indo-Pacific lives the blue-striped cleaner wrasse. As its name suggests, this species, with an elongated body adorned with electric blue stripes, provides a service for other reef inhabitants. Lurking in the vicinity, however, is a fish of more dubious character: the bluestriped fangblenny. The fangblenny looks the spitting image of the wrasse, so much so that clients come to it to be cleaned; instead, they receive a nasty surprise. The fangblenny gets its name from the sharp teeth it possesses, which it uses to bite chunks of flesh out of those fish visiting for a service. It disguises itself as a helpful cleaner fish, but actually intends only to take bites out of the visitors.

The fangblenny is also capable of changing colour, morphing to orange or dull brown colours when needed. This affords another route to a meal, since the fangblenny can now insert itself into shoals of passing fish, seizing the opportunity to take chunks out of them too. To achieve this, fangblennies can mimic a variety of fish, but they do not have it all their own way. At the cleaning station, their very nature is costly not only to the visiting clients,

In the Maldives, the bright blue stripes on a bluestreak cleaner wrasse signal to clients the service it offers.

An imposter – the bluestriped fangblenny from the Great Barrier Reef, Australia, uses its disguise to attack fish.

but to the cleaner fish as well. Reef fish that have experienced a negative interaction at the site where the fangblenny is located will begin to avoid it. They can learn that this is not a station to be trusted, but rather one to avoid. When this starts to happen, the fangblenny will switch back to darting out at fish swimming by, seizing any opportunity to get its food, or, it may move off to a new station to exploit.

The fangblenny is not the only reef fish that uses deception to obtain a meal. Other tricksters are even more dangerous. Blissfully unaware of the threat from within their group, a school of juvenile brown damselfish swim along a coral reef off the Queensland coast. Their dull colour is matched by an intruder, the dusky dottyback. Seemingly safe in the presence of one of their own kind, the damselfish get closer and end up as dinner for the dottyback. Sooner or later, the damselfish catch on to the deadly insider and the dottyback must look elsewhere for prey. A group of juvenile yellow damselfish makes the ideal place. But the dottyback cannot outwit them just yet. First, over a series of days, it must change colour, turning from a dull brown to a bright yellow to blend in. With its disguise complete, the dottyback can now feast on unsuspecting damselfish once more.

When fish on the reef get wise to the tricks of bluestriped fangblennies, the imposters must find targets elsewhere.

BEHIND THE SCIENCE

The use of mimicry has important implications in nature and for how evolution actually works. One of the reasons is that the presence of a mimic carries a cost, not just to those animals that it is trying to deceive, but also to those creatures that are being mimicked in the first place (the 'model'). For example, hoverflies are completely harmless to birds, but many avian predators avoid them. The bird loses a meal as a result, but the wasps or bees being mimicked may also pay a price. At times during their lives, predators will sample prey, even those that they might consider as dangerous and normally worth avoiding. This is especially true when a predator is young and relatively naïve. Should a bird sample a hoverfly, it would learn that this insect is harmless and palatable. As a result, the bird may be encouraged to attack more hoverflies, and also attack bees and wasps – after all, they may be harmless too, since the hoverfly coloration is a con. So the presence of mimics can create a potential burden for the creatures they resemble.

The relationship between hoverfly mimics and, for example, wasp models can depend on how common they are relative to one another. If the hoverflies become too common, the chances are that more and more predators will sample them and start to see through the disguise. In turn, attacks on wasps also rise. There becomes a risk that the whole mimicry system may break down, or at least fluctuate in effectiveness over time. So, in evolutionary terms, there's a delicate balance between how common mimics are relative to their models, and, ideally, they should be rarer. In some cases, the dangerous insect may be driven to evolve a different colour form to 'escape' the burden of its mimics.

Another solution, adopted by many mimics, is to come in several forms. For example, if some look like a certain bee but others like a wasp, then the chances of lots of predators breaking their disguise are lessened. A further consideration is just how dangerous the model is. A particularly ferocious hornet may rarely be attacked, since the cost to a bold predator may be great. In turn, a higher number of hornet-mimicking flies may persist, since they are better protected owing to the level of defence their model affords them.

Sometimes, the deception used by predators to lure prey can be so breath-taking as to send tingles down your spine. In the mountains of western Iran resides a snake, the spider-tailed horned viper, whose mimicry is on a whole other level, and a deadly one too. This snake, which until recently had been seldom seen and barely studied, carries at the tip of its tail a curious appendage: a bulbous structure, flanked by small elongated scales. For many years the nature of the tail arrangement was a mystery; perhaps simply a mutation or developmental error producing an unusual growth in the single specimen that had been studied. Then, recently, scientists managed to film the snake hunting, and its deadly outcome. The viper, beautifully camouflaged against the rocky habitat, gently sways its tail in a small arc from side to side. As it does so, it creates the unmistakable impression of a large juicy spider with an abdomen and legs running back and forth. A warbler flies down, pecks at the pseudo-spider and in a flash the bird is grabbed by the snake. The use of an appendage, often the tail or tongue, to lure prey is not uncommon in reptiles. A few other snakes, such as the Saharan sand viper, also adopt this route,

though not so convincingly as in the example above. The sand viper lies partly buried, with the tip of its tail sticking out of the sand, wriggling somewhat like an insect larva.

For certain creatures, luring prey is one of the best ways to obtain food that would otherwise be difficult to capture. The alligator snapping turtle from North America is a beast of a reptile. Weighing upwards of 70 kilograms, this giant would struggle to pursue most active prey. Instead, the turtle is capable of staying underwater for well over half an hour, and it rarely ventures onto dry land. It is not a fussy eater, consuming a variety of fish, amphibians, invertebrates and even birds and other turtles. When below the surface, the turtle lies in wait, its mouth open, ready to crunch down with incredible force onto anything that comes close. The end of its tongue is specially modified, with a bright pink fleshy appendage filled with blood. It is hard to escape

*An aptly named spider-tailed horned viper in Iran eagerly waits
for an inquisitive bird to visit.*

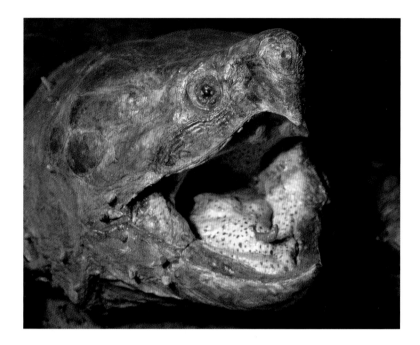

the assumption that this has evolved to mimic a juicy worm. Sure enough, a host of prey animals, especially fish, are drawn to the turtle's jaws by making this mistake.

* * *

Staying alive and finding food are critical tasks for most organisms, but ultimately their evolutionary success is judged by how well they reproduce and pass on their genes. Naturally, some creatures don't play fair in order to get ahead of the game. In parts of northern Europe and Asia breeds a bird called a ruff. The name is an apt one for this shorebird, since most males display to females with the sort of elaborate neck plumage that looked fashionable in Britain during the reign of Elizabeth I. In a similar way to birds like black grouse and peacocks, males

The crushing jaws of an alligator snapping turtle are baited with a wiggling 'worm'.

usually display to females in a lek system, with females choosing the male with which they are most impressed. A small number of males also hangs out around the edges, hoping to procure mating opportunities without putting in the hard work.

Things are not entirely as they seem, however, for lurking in among all the others is another group of males that look very different. They lack the dark plumage and obvious ruff, are smaller than most males and look suspiciously like females. These males are sneakers – they embed themselves within the groups, pretending to be female, so that the sneaker can attempt to quickly grab an opportunity to mate with a willing female when a dominant male's back is turned. Sneaky males make up just 1 per cent of the entire male population, presumably because, rather like hoverflies and other Batesian mimics, were they to be too common then everyone else would tune in to their deception. By going incognito like this, they can achieve

Male ruff birds display and fight on a lek in Finland. Unseen, other female-like males take a different route to mating success.

some degree of mating success, without the effort of fighting off rival males and having to display.

Endemic to South Africa, the Augrabies flat lizard lives in the rocky countryside and around waterfalls, where the lizards perform acrobatic jumps to catch blackfly. It is perhaps the most colourful reptile on the whole planet, or at least most of the males are. While females are a dull brown, mature males have a head and back ornamented with bright shiny green–blue, front legs covered in yellow and hind limbs of orange.

Male Augrabies lizards perform dances and displays to compete with rivals for good territories and the affection of females, adopting strange postures to show off their colours and vitality. Should the displays fail, fights may break out, which can sometimes do significant harm to the loser. In between bouts of displaying, the lizards must feed, and so, while the ornamented males are preoccupied with jumping for flies, another type of male tries his

Male Augrabies flat lizards display their colours to one another as a way of defending their territory and to compete for females.

luck with the females. He is drab brown and inconspicuous, and looks just like a female. But he doesn't smell like one, and if he can get close enough to a real female then there is a chance she will know he is a male and accept him for a mate. It's a risky strategy, however, since, if the sneaker male gets too close to a rival, he will be aggressively attacked and chased away.

Sneaker strategies are not uncommon in nature, when there is intense competition for mates. In the case of the Augrabies lizards it is a temporary strategy, used only by younger males that have yet to develop the strength and skills required to compete outright for territories and potential partners. When they fully grow up, their ornamentation develops too, and sneaking is no longer an option.

Cuttlefish may be masters of concealment, but they also use their incredible colour-changing skills for another sort of deception, this time in mating displays. Males must court females in order to mate, but face the challenge of other males continuously muscling in on the action and spoiling their chances. Remarkably, male mourning cuttlefish, living in

A male mourning cuttlefish displays to a female, while simultaneously adopting a female appearance on the other side of his body.

Australia's Sydney Harbour, counteract this by splitting their bodies down the middle and adopting a different uniform on each side. On the side facing the female, a male shows typical pulsating mating displays, whereas on the side facing outwards, seen by potential rivals, he adopts a colour scheme more reminiscent of another female. To another male, it looks like two females. It's a tricky skill to balance, though, since, when more individuals are around, he risks sending the wrong message to multiple parties, spoiling his chances and attracting the ire of rivals, so this half-and-half deception is used only in small groups. Cuttlefish, like other cephalopods, have high levels of ability when it comes to decision-making, and the brains to know when to adopt different tactics that are most likely to succeed given the circumstances.

* * *

For those animals that raise their young, the task is often one of the most demanding that they must perform at any point in their lives. Looking out for danger, building a nest, spending great time and energy going out to look for food to bring back to the young, all exert considerable strain on parents. But what if a parent could get someone else to do all the hard work? A variety of animals do and, for them, the key to tricking others into raising their offspring often lies in the use of colour.

In the countryside of Britain, the unmistakable sound of the common cuckoo can be heard off in the distance, a sign of spring and early summer. Close by, a female cuckoo sits perched in a tree, hidden from all but the keenest eyes. She has no desire to be seen, especially not by the mother robin who is building a nest down below. The cuckoo monitors the robin's breeding efforts, waiting for eggs to appear. Then, when the nest is unguarded, the cuckoo swoops down, before flying off just a few minutes later. In this short time, she has performed a devious task, for inside the nest there are still four eggs, lightly coloured with brown speckles, but now, one is a little larger than the others. In her brief visit, the cuckoo removed one of the robin's eggs and laid her own; the forgery is a wonderfully close match to the colour and pattern of the robin's own eggs. The cuckoo, her part in the life of this unhatched chick now done, heads off to visit other potential victims. She is a type of bird that is often called a 'brood parasite', tricking others into rearing her young.

On returning to the nest, the mother robin dutifully incubates the eggs and, after a few days, the larger one is the first to hatch. The chick begs vociferously, willing its foster parents to supply it with food. It also has other plans: while the adult birds are away, it begins to heave the remaining eggs onto its back, lifting them up and dropping them to the ground below. Now, alone in the nest, the cuckoo chick can monopolise all the care and, before fledging, grow to a size much greater than an adult robin.

Not all robins are so compliant. Many potential foster parents, coming from a variety of host species, fight back against the cuckoo's wily ways. In turn, the cuckoo has evolved an arsenal of tricks to get ahead of the game, like an arms race between two warring parties. The cuckoo's first task is to gain access to the nest unnoticed. Should she fail and be detected, the hosts will mob and even physically attack her, driving her away. Indeed, many potential host birds are alert to the threats that a cuckoo brings, and they heighten their wariness when there is cause for extra caution, not least a recently spotted cuckoo. Reed warblers nesting in the fenlands of East Anglia will, for example, show much stronger defensive behaviours to cuckoos when they have recently seen one nearby.

The parasite has a method to stop the hosts in their tracks, however. To begin with, she is elusive, rarely seen close up, but instead preferring to lurk in the vegetation and trees, where she can watch nests in secret. And there's more. Inspect a cuckoo closely and you may note some familiar features: a grey-brown general appearance, white breast with striking dark barring patterns, and yellow and orange eyes. One could be forgiven for thinking that there was a sparrowhawk sitting in the tree, and this is exactly what the cuckoo intends. Even its flight is strikingly hawk-like. If there is one thing that a small bird should generally not do, it is to try to mob a deadly hawk. By resembling a bird of prey, the hosts not only fail to realise that it is their clutch which is under threat rather than them, but they even flee the nest to escape the apparent danger, leaving the nest unguarded. The need to avoid being eaten is strong; many birds will even show strong avoidance of a wood pigeon painted with black bars on their breast feathers.

Should the cuckoo break through this first line of defence, all is not yet lost. Many potential host birds will spot the forgery

The large size of a common cuckoo egg is a giveaway, but the reed warbler parents seem to rarely notice, focusing on the colour patterns instead.

and reject eggs that seem out of place before they hatch. Mostly, this is based on the cuckoo egg failing to closely match the colours and patterns of the host's own eggs. It is this very selection pressure that has driven the common cuckoo to evolve egg mimicry in the first place. To be successful, cuckoos must defeat the hosts' defences, and that means outwitting the keen eyes of the birds they are trying to dupe.

There is, though, even more to this story. Each mother cuckoo specialises in laying her eggs in the nests of a specific host species, but not all cuckoos target the same ones. Some common cuckoos target robins, others reed warblers, dunnocks, bramblings, and so on. The common cuckoo has been found to regularly exploit at least half a dozen species in the UK, but will from time to time lay its eggs in many others. Worldwide, it may utilise several hundred hosts, albeit many only on occasions. Generally speaking, each of those cuckoos that target one of the primary foster-carer species has eggs that mimic those of their favoured host. In fact, it is more nuanced than this because it also depends on how discerning the hosts are. Bramblings, for example, are very discriminating, and so cuckoos that target those birds must have eggs that resemble those of a brambling very closely. By contrast, dunnocks do not reject foreign eggs at all; they may be a relatively new host, evolutionarily speaking, and so cuckoos have no need to match the blue eggs of a dunnock because whatever eggs they lay will be accepted. In short, host birds that are more discriminating in telling apart their own eggs from those of a cuckoo have forced those cuckoos to evolve better egg mimicry.

Given the obvious benefits of tricking others into rearing your offspring, it is perhaps surprising that only 1 per cent of the world's birds are brood parasites. Part of the reason is that, as we know, some hosts fight back, and so success rates are not always as high as we might first imagine. Not only that, but, while most birds can get straight into building a nest, a mother cuckoo must scope out potential victims and wait for the opportune moments to lay her eggs in those nests. Nonetheless, brood parasitism has evolved at least seven times independently among the birds, so it must be a way of living that is worth it in many cases. On the other hand, host birds can sometimes develop defences that are so good that they nearly always win against the parasite. In those cases, when the parasite has had to evolve egg markings closely matched to that host and can no longer raise her own young, the parasite is stuck and cannot breed. It is perhaps for this reason that brood parasites are also more likely to go extinct over time than birds that raise their own young.

* * *

The story of the common cuckoo was once thought to be representative of most brood parasite interactions across the world, but we now know that there are plenty of departures from this. In the outback of Australia lives the large-billed gerygone. When nesting, it builds an enclosed dome nest, in which its white eggs are nestled in the darkness. Gerygones are targeted by the little bronze cuckoo, which surprisingly makes little effort to match the colour of the host eggs. Instead, the cuckoo egg is a dark muddy brown, so thickly coated in pigment that some of it can be wiped off. The cuckoo egg is well camouflaged in the nest, such that it is hard for a host bird to see that there is one there at all, so gerygones seldom reject cuckoo eggs. This might be because the gerygones have never had the opportunity to evolve rejection behaviour. But, there is probably another reason for the cryptic cuckoo eggs, and that is other cuckoos. In locations where the cuckoos are common, each

Overleaf: In spite of its enormous size, the reed warbler parent still finds the begging calls of a cuckoo chick irresistible.

gerygone can be targeted by more than one nest parasite. Yet no cuckoo wants its own young to have to compete with the young of another cuckoo as well. Like most brood parasites, when she lays her egg, a mother cuckoo will therefore remove one of the eggs already in the nest, and, when doing so, it benefits her most to remove the egg of another cuckoo. By laying dark camouflaged eggs, however, each little bronze cuckoo can reduce the chance that its egg will be seen and removed by a competitor.

Australia is home to a large number of the world's brood parasites, and some of the most remarkable adaptations. Perhaps because the nests of many cuckoo hosts are dark, few of the hosts have evolved egg rejection behaviour; it would be too error prone and haphazard, with the hosts unable to see the differences well enough to do so accurately. They risk throwing their own eggs out by mistake. Instead, it has recently been discovered that hosts of several species of Australian bronze cuckoos reject not the eggs, but the cuckoo chicks. One such host, the superb fairywren, will abandon a lone Horsfield's bronze cuckoo chick left in its nest, leaving the chick to die. After all, given that the cuckoo chick evicts the host's own eggs, being left with one chick is a sign to the foster parents of something untoward. Yet some host species are more discriminating and can save their brood before it is too late. Several species of gerygone, targeted by the little bronze cuckoo, actively pick up and throw the freshly hatched cuckoo chick from the nest. Even more remarkably, the cuckoos have fought back, with cuckoos that target different host birds having chicks that bear a striking resemblance to the coloration of the host chicks, including with black, yellow or pink skin tones. Just like egg mimicry by the common cuckoo in Europe, it's a trick to fool the discriminating eyes of the hosts. Even more recently, mimicry of host chicks has been found in some of the little studied birds of New Guinea. It is probably more common than we realise.

Brood parasites have two challenges that arise from the way that they hand over their breeding to others. Beating the host's defences is the first of these but, once a cuckoo chick has been accepted, it has another task – it must extract as much food and care from its foster parents as it can manage, in order to grow big and strong before fledging. Since many cuckoos parasitise hosts that would normally be much smaller than themselves, a cuckoo chick must find ways of encouraging the hosts to feed them. This is important, since host birds might normally decrease the amount of food they bring to the nest if they have just one chick to provision, rather than supply the amount they would provide for a full clutch of, say, four young.

Chicks of the common cuckoo are well known to beg extremely strongly; those that target reed warblers, for instance, use exaggerated vocal displays that resemble a brood of four host chicks. They also have vivid red mouth colours. Other cuckoos use even more incredible visual tricks. Around two to three thousand metres up on the slopes of Mount Fuji in Japan lives the Japanese Horsfield's hawk cuckoo. It is uncommon and, like most cuckoos, elusive. It targets birds like the bluetail, which nests in small dark holes on the volcanic mountain sides. In the thick forest, the light is dim and the nest gloomy. Bluetail nests are also heavily targeted by predators, with most breeding attempts unsuccessful, so a cuckoo chick cannot afford a loud begging display, else it too will end up as a meal. Instead, when the bluetail parents come to feed the chick, the cuckoo raises one wing, showing a bright yellow patch on the underside, which is striking in the gloom, and embarks on a bout of frenzied begging. The wing patches have evolved to resemble the mouth of the young, also a bright yellow, and trick the hosts that there is not one, but two or even three chicks in the nest. As a result, they bring more food to the growing parasite. The light conditions are not only gloomy, but also rich in scattered ultraviolet light, owing to the high-altitude conditions where the birds live. Birds can see these wavelengths of light and, to heighten their sense of awareness of the wing patch, the yellow also reflects ultraviolet light strongly.

Africa also has its fair share of parasitic birds, including the vidua finches. These birds lay their eggs in the nests of other types of finch, and both birds have stunning mouth colours. In some cases, the inside of the mouth shows off black spots, while the rim is ornamented with glowing blue or white bumps. It is most likely that these mouth colours evolved in the host chicks some time before they were under threat from parasites, because the many species of finch that are not – and are likely never to have been – parasitised also have such markings. Instead, they probably first evolved to act as signals to the host parents, indicating which chicks are in the best condition. It stimulates the parents to bring more provisions and, as much as anything, shows them where to place the food. Consequently, the parasitic vidua finches had to evolve mouth markings that closely resembled those of the host chicks, else they would miss out on the food being provided. In turn, this may have led to an arms race, with the hosts evolving more elaborate mouth markings to gain more food, especially when at risk of being parasitised, and the vidua chicks following suit to keep up. The ultimate result is a diversity of glowing mouth markings.

Deception may be assumed as the providence of animals, but that is far from the truth. It abounds in plants and fungi as well, often involving tricks of light and colour. Chief among these are the orchids, where one-third of all orchid species (a group of around 30,000) entice pollinating insects without offering any sort of reward for their services. In a fairer arrangement, most flowers provide a tip for pollinators, usually nectar or some of the nutritious pollen itself. Yet deceptive orchids forego this part of the arrangement. That means, without a reward to offer, the orchid flowers must entice insects with other false promises.

Although bee orchids are self-fertile in the UK, in other parts of the world their flowers are pollinated by male bees. The insects are duped into mistaking the flowers as female bees, on account not only of their colour but also their scent, which resembles female 'come hither' pheromones. In the process of trying to mate with the flower, the bee collects pollen and then transports it to the next plant, whose appeal it can't resist. They're traits shared by many species in the orchid family. They present the colours of potential mates and so entice bees and wasps into the false prospect of a mating opportunity. Other plants trick pollinators in a similar manner. The South African daisy flower is marked with dark bumps on some of its petals, which to male flies look rather like a female ready to mate. The fly wastes time and energy trying to mate with the flower, which is pollinated as a result. In time, flies can learn to avoid the flowers, and this has, in turn, driven the daisies to evolve lots of different colour types, from yellow to orange or red and marked with varied patterns, such that the bees are consistently tricked.

Deception is not just used by plants for reproduction. Carnivorous plants tend to live in places or niches where they struggle to obtain sufficient nutrients. Many have evolved a variety of wily ways to supplement their diet with invertebrate

prey. The plants can often be elegant and beautiful. The sundew plants, which grow in boggy marshland, have bright red structures glistening with sticky liquid to ensnare anything small that walks on them. Pitcher plants can create long tubes, marked with white veins or red coloration, which often seem to glow with the light that passes through them. The tubes of pitcher plants are filled with digestive liquid, and have a slippery rim at the top. Insects that climb up to the edge of the pitcher or land on it, fall off the rim and down into the trap below. In some pitcher plants, the rims fluoresce, emitting a pale blue light that is attractive to flies and other insects. Rather like the Australian crab spider, the plant lures prey with colours that glow and are irresistible to the vision of flies and other creatures. Various pitcher plants, as well as the famous Venus fly trap with its

Venus fly traps are the iconic carnivorous plant, their traps triggered when a prey animal trips the hairs inside, as did this wasp.

The glistening red of a sundew plant from the Isle of Mull, Scotland.

spring-loaded cages, entice insects that are attracted to the bright red colours that they develop.

Plants are not alone in playing tricks. Fungi do too. One fungus found in Brazil and referred to as the 'coconut flower' emits an eerie green bioluminescent light at night. The glow is controlled by a circadian rhythm in the fungus and is only switched on at night, when it is dark. By glowing green, the fungus has evolved a strategy to lure insects towards it. They wander over the fungus, picking up spores that they then spread far and wide. Other plants and fungi use deceptions of a different nature, often focused on chemicals rather than − or in addition to − colour, but there are likely to be many more cases of visual deception used by these organisms waiting to be discovered.

* * *

Deception in nature takes many guises and works in a rich variety of ways. While we might often talk of cheats in nature, evolution has no real rulebook regarding what's allowed and what isn't in order to be successful, and no foresight, consciousness or planning ahead. What ultimately matters is staying alive and passing on your genes in reproduction. If that can be achieved through trickery and disguise, then so be it. Playing fair is often hard, dangerous or time-consuming, and all kinds of creatures will adopt deceptive behaviours and colour forms if it helps them to stay alive, find food and breed. However, there is frequently a delicate balance here, since, if too many cheats arise, then the system can break down, and animals may learn to avoid those that don't play fair. All this adds to the selection pressure placed on tricksters to enhance and refine their costumes, such that they continue to work effectively in a world of sceptics. In many regards, this has led to some of the most remarkable examples of adaptation in nature, from birds that mimic caterpillars, to insects that resemble flowers. Evolution it seems, likes a good con artist.

Some plants and fungi, like these from the southeast Atlantic Forest, Brazil, fluoresce under ultraviolet light.

South African daisy flowers form carpets in the spring, the raised dark bumps attracting male flies that try to mate with them.

INDEX

ACKNOWLEDGEMENTS

There are a great many people who have made both the book and TV series possible, including a large number of scientists and research organisations, field stations and wildlife experts. Their advice and input has been invaluable in discovering and making the stories come to life.

The success of the TV series is also thanks to the hard work and dedication of a wonderful production team, film crew, and range of assistants and researchers behind the scenes.

I'd like to sincerely thank Stephen Dunleavy and Sharmila Choudhury at Humble Bee Films as well as Colette Beaudry and Adam Geiger at SeaLight Pictures for getting me involved in this project. In particular, Sharmila has given valuable feedback on the chapters and guidance throughout. It has been a pleasure working together.

Great thanks go to Michael Bright for his considerable input with the writing of the book, Laura Barwick for finding so many wonderful images to include, and all the team at Penguin Random House for their guidance and input throughout, in order to make a book that, by the very nature of the subject, needed to be so striking and visual.

Finally, I would like to thank friends and family for their considerable support, encouragement and enthusiasm throughout the entire project. It would not be possible without them.

Martin Stevens
Professor of Sensory and Evolutionary Ecology

The production of *Life in Colour* was a collaboration between Humble Bee Films in the UK and SeaLight Pictures in Australia.

We are indebted to the many scientists across the globe studying the role of colour in the natural world. The generosity of their time and their enthusiasm for our series made it all possible. As well as scientists sharing stories of their research, we were guided in our scientific storytelling by Professor Justin Marshall. His expert knowledge on the use of colour in nature was invaluable.

Justin and his colleague Dr Sam Powell also helped devise and create wonderful camera systems for visualising a world of colour that lies beyond our eyes. These systems were crucial to helping tell the full picture of life in colour. And in this we must also thank Professor Viktor Gruev for his work developing technology to help to reveal the world of polarisation.

As well as the scientists, we must thank the cinematographers, drone operators, fixers and all the specialist technical teams who helped capture the magnificence of colour. They were ably guided and supported by our small but dedicated production teams in both the UK and Australia, who worked tirelessly over the two years of production.

Finally, we owe a big thank you to Sir David Attenborough for wanting to make this series in the first place, more than 60 years after he made his first series on the subject of colour and patterns in animals.

Stephen Dunleavy & Colette Beaudry
Executive Producers

Presented by
Sir David Attenborough

Executive Producers
Stephen Dunleavy,
  Humble Bee Films
Colette Beaudry,
  SeaLight Pictures

**Humble Bee Films
Production Team**
Sharmila Choudhury
Bridget Appleby
Clare Bean
Steve Clark
Tamara Collin
Helen Drew
Nick Green
Ashwika Kapur
Natalie Mycielski
Guthrie O'Brien
Samuel Smithers
Carina Thomas
Sally Thomson
Lisa Walters
Debbie Williams
Elena Wong

**SeaLight Pictures
Production Team**
Adam Geiger
Stephen Boyle
Michael Drake
Leah Hall
Rebecca Humphries
Carolyn Johnson
Alice Orszulok
Annabel Robinson

Camera Crew
Adam Akradi
Barrie Britton
John Brown
Robin Cox
Benjamin Cunningham
Vianet Djenguet
John Duncan
Jason Elliott
Richard Fitzpatrick
Adam Geiger
Graham Hatherley
Richard Hill
Max Hug Williams
Alex Jones
Joao Krajewski
Tim Laman
Mark Lamble
Stuart Lamble
Katie Mayhew
Cam McGrath
Rory McGuinness
Chris Miller
Sean Miller
Michael O'Reilly
Mark Payne-Gill
Bill Rudolph

Edwin Scholes
Daniel Stoupin
Gavin Thurston
Jamie Unwin
Kalyan Varma
Pete West
Mark Yates

Music
James Dorman

Editors
Angela Maddick
Andy Netley
Tim Lasseter
David Warner
Stephen Barnes
Bobby Sheikh
Mark Fox

Post Production Team
Vince Brant
Simon Buckton-Collins
Jonathan Cawte
Annelie Chapple
Andy Devine
Paul Fisher
Rose Georgiana
Angela Groves
Wes Hibberd
Richard Hinton
Brian Moseley
Christian Short
Graham Wild
Films @59 Bristol – Patsy
  Hayden & Bobby Tutton
Big Bang Sydney – Libby
  Villa & Wayne Pashley
Blue Post Sydney – Rachel
  Knowles & Adam Archer
BDH visual effects

With Special Thanks
Jordi Canut Bartra
Alejandro Bello
Chris Castles
Marie Charpentier
Jim Cornfoot
Fabio Cortesi
Molly Cummings
Oscar Cuso
Simon Dunn
John Fennell
Adrian Gonzalez Guillen
Viktor Gruev
Tom Hartwell
Mariella Herberstein
Martin How
Gabriel Jamie
Darrell Kemp
Thomas Koblinger
Justin Marshall
Claudio Mettke-Hofmann
Scott Mills
Ian Morris
Oli Neilson

Julio Nunez
Sam Oakes
Sam Powell
Julian Renoult
Bernardo Reyes-Tur
Paul Rose
Graeme Sawyer
Richard Simpson
Martin Stevens
Laszlo Talas
Lisa Taylor
Bryson Voirin
Martin Whiting
Joerg Wiedenmann
Yusan Yang
Augrabies Falls National Park
Australian Butterfly Sanctuary
Australian Museum Lizard
  Island Reef Research
  Station
Boyd Deep Canyon Desert
  Research Center
Cairngorm Mountain
Coffs Harbour Butterfly
  House
CONAF
Cornell Laboratory of
  Ornithology
Heron Island Research
  Station
Karnataka Forest Department
La Paz Waterfall Gardens
La Selva Research Station
Macquarie University
  Department of Biological
  Sciences
Mandrillus Project
Mara North Conservancy
Mills Laboratory, University
  of Montana
Moreton Bay Research
  Station
Queensland Brain Institute,
  University of Queensland
Sydney Institute of Marine
  Science
The Crown Estate
The Royal Parks
Tiskita Jungle Lodge
University of Bristol
University of California,
  Riverside

**Production Funding
& Support**
The British Broadcasting
  Corporation
Netflix Inc
Nine Network Australia
Stan Entertainment
Screen Australia
Screen New South Wales
Screen Queensland
Flame Distribution

PICTURE CREDITS

1 Alex Hyde; **2-3** Nick Garbutt; **4** Alex Mustard; **7** Loop Images Ltd/Alamy; **8** David Hall/naturepl.com; **10-11** Greg Basco/BIA/naturepl.com; **13** Nick Garbutt

Chapter 1 FRIEND OR FOE
16-19 Reinhard Dirscherl/FLPA; **20t** Colin Marshall/FLPA; **20b, 21t** Gary Bell/Oceanwide/naturepl.com; **21b** WaterFrame/Alamy; **24** Cyril Ruoso/naturepl.com; **28tl** Suzi Eszterhas/naturepl.com; **28tr** Gerard Lacz/FLPA; **28bl** Cyril Ruoso/naturepl.com; **28br** Imagebroker/Alamy; **30** blickwinkel/Alamy; **32-2** Michael Sheehan; **35** Ronald Moolenaar/Minden/FLPA; **36** Pascal Pittorino/naturepl.com; **37** Henry Firus; **38-9** Marko Konig/Imagebroker/FLPA; **42** Colin Marshall/FLPA; **44** Humble Bee Films; **47** Jonathan M. Douglas; **51** Humble Bee Films; **52** Thomas Marent/Minden/FLPA; **55** Tim Laman/Nat Geo Image Collection/naturepl.com

Chapter 2 ATTRACTING MATES
58t Kevin Elsby/FLPA; **58b** Alex Mustard/naturepl.com; **61** Klein & Hubert/naturepl.com; **62** David Kjaer/naturepl.com; **66-7** Theo Webb/naturepl.com; **69** Joseph Schubert; **71-2** Michael Doe; **74** Humble Bee Films; **77** Nick Garbutt; **79-80** Humble Bee Films; **82** Martin Willis/Minden/naturepl.com; **83** Dakota E. McCoy; **85** Nick Garbutt; **89** Robert Heathcote; **91** Dhritiman Mukherjee; **94** Xi Zhinong/naturepl.com; **96-7** Tim Laman; **99** Kevin Schafer/Minden/naturepl.com; **100** Matthias Breiter/Minden/naturepl.com; **102** Imagebroker/FLPA; **103** Roger Powell/naturepl.com

Chapter 3 DOMINANCE & RIVALRY
109 Denis-Huot/naturepl.com; **110-1** Martin Dohrn/naturepl.com; **113** Denis-Huot/naturepl.com; **114-5** Juan Carlos Munoz/naturepl.com; **117** Mark MacEwen/naturepl.com; **119** Guthrie O'Brien/Humble Bee Films; **122** Ingo Arndt/naturepl.com; **125** Alex Hyde; **126-7** Nick Garbutt; **130-1** Martin Willis/Minden/naturepl.com; **133** Kevin Bauman**; 134** Jane Burton/naturepl.com; **135** Alex Hyde; **139** Edward Myles/FLPA; **142t** David Fleetham/naturepl.com; **142b** Georgette Douwma/naturepl.com; **144** Humble Bee Films; **147** Thomas Ozanne/Getty; **148-9** Humble Bee Films

Chapter 4 WARNING SIGNALS
154 Jason Ondreicka/Alamy; **156** Humble Bee Films; **158-9** Mark Moffett/Minden/naturepl.com; **163t** AGAMI Photo Agency/Alamy; **163b** Daniel Heuclin/naturepl.com; **166-7** Cyril Ruoso/naturepl.com; **169** Visuals Unlimited/naturepl.com; **170t** Colin Varndell/naturepl.com; **170b** Brian Lightfoot/naturepl.com; **174** Alex Hyde; **176-7** Norma Jean Gargasz/Alamy; **181** Juan Carlos Munoz/naturepl.com; **182t** Chien C. Lee; **182b** Dietmar Nill/naturepl.com; **183t** Robert Thompson/naturepl.com; **183b** Greg M Walter; **187** Martin Stevens; **188t** Alex Mustard/naturepl.com; **88b** Doug Perrine/naturepl.com; **190** Alex Mustard/2020VISION/naturepl.com; **191** Gary Nafis; **193** imageBROKER/Alamy; **194-5** Pete Oxford/Minden/naturepl.com; **197t** Geoff Scott-Simpson/naturepl.com; **197b** Chien C. Lee; **200** Shane Gross/naturepl.com; **202** Tony Heald; **203** Sylvain Cordier/naturepl.com

Chapter 5 CAMOUFLAGE
206tl Brandon Cole/naturepl.com; **206tr** Jurgen Freund/naturepl.com; **206b** Alex Mustard; **208-9** Humble Bee Films; **213** Guy Edwardes/naturepl.com; **216t** Fogden/Minden/Alamy; **216b** Reinhard Dirscherl/imageBROKER/imagequestmarine.com; **218** Karin Rothman/Minden/FLPA; **219** Andy Murch/imagequestmarine.com; **220** Wild Wonders of Europe/Pitkin/naturepl.com; **222** Alex Mustard; **223** Emanuele Biggi/naturepl.com; **224t** Alex Hyde; **224b** Robert Thompson/naturepl.com; **227** MindenPictures/Alamy; **228** Alex Mustard; **229** Martin Stevens; **231** Nature Photographers Ltd/Alamy; **232t** Nick Hawkins/naturepl.com; **232b** Alex Mustard; **235** Wild Wonders Europe/Lundgren/naturepl.com; **240-3** Humble Bee Films; **244** Marko Beric/Alamy; **247** Nick Greaves/Alamy; **250-1** Espen Bergerson/naturepl.com; **254t** Joao Burini/naturepl.com; **254b** Stephen Dalton/naturepl.com; **256** Denis-Huot/naturepl.com; **259** Emanuele Biggi/naturepl.com

Chapter 6 DECEPTION
263 Alex Hyde; **264** Sinclair Stammers/Science Photo Library; **267** Rod Williams/naturepl.com; **268** Alex Hyde; **269** Mark Moffett/Minden/naturepl.com; **271** Nick Garbutt; **274tl** Visuals Unlimited/naturepl.com; **274tr** Ross Hoddinott/2020VISION/naturepl.com; **274b** Felipe B. R. Gomes; **276** David Fleetham/naturepl.com; **278** Visuals Unlimited/naturepl.com; **279** Solvin Zankl/naturepl.com; **281** Humble Bee Films; **283** Andy Sands/naturepl.com; **284** Alex Hyde; **287t** incamerastock/Alamy; **287b** Gary Bell/Oceanwide/naturepl.com; **288** Norbert Wu/Minden/naturepl.com; **292** Matthijs Kuijpers/Alamy; **293** Scott Camazine/Alamy; **294** Loic Poidevin/naturepl.com; **295** Humble Bee Films; **296** Marty Garwood; **298** blickwinkel/Alamy; **300-1** imageBROKER/Alamy; **308** Chris Mattison/naturepl.com; **309** Nick Garbutt; **310t** Joao Burini/naturepl.com; **310b** Fogden/Minden/Alamy

endpaper *front* Georgette Douwma/naturepl.com; **endpaper** *back* Alex Hyde

Witness Books, an imprint of Ebury Publishing
20 Vauxhall Bridge Road, London SW1V 2SA

Witness Books is part of the Penguin Random House
group of companies whose addresses can be found
at global.penguinrandomhouse.com

Penguin
Random House
UK

This book is published to accompany the television
series entitled *Life in Colour*, first broadcast on
BBC One in 2021.

Executive producers: Stephen Dunleavy and Colette Beaudry
Series producer: Sharmila Choudhury

First published by Witness Books in 2021

www.penguin.co.uk

A CIP catalogue record for this book is available from the
British Library

978-1-785-94637-0

Publishing Director: Albert DePetrillo
Project Editor: Nell Warner
Picture Research: Laura Barwick
Image Grading: Stephen Johnson, www.copyrightimage.co.uk
Design: Bobby Birchall, Bobby&Co
Production: Antony Heller

Printed and bound in Italy by L.E.G.O. S.p.A

Penguin Random House is committed to a sustainable future
for our business, our readers and our planet. This book is made
from Forest Stewardship Council® certified paper.

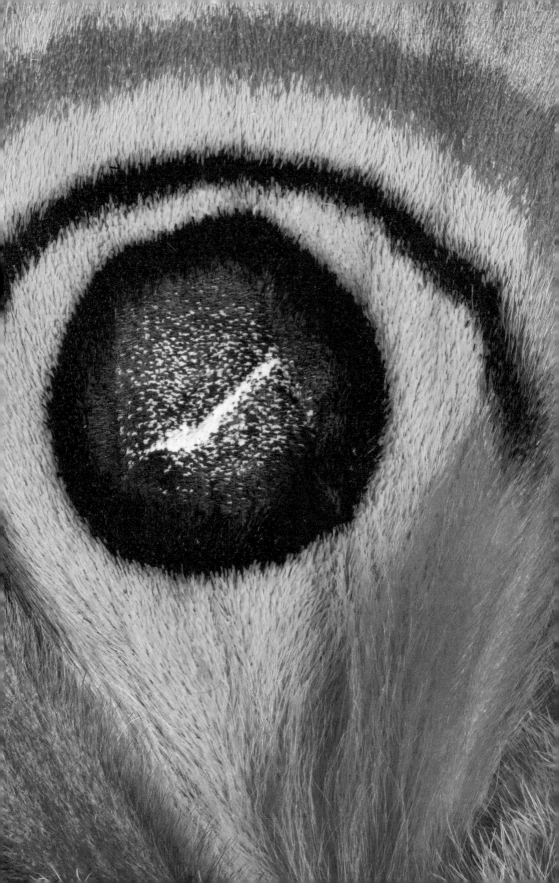